D1605941

ILLINOIS STUDIES IN

THE SOCIAL SCIENCES

VOLUME XXXIII

CONTENTS

Open Door Diplomat

Open Door Diplomat

The Life of W. W. Rockhill

PAUL A. VARG

ILLINOIS STUDIES IN THE SOCIAL SCIENCES: *Volume* XXXIII, *No. 4*

GREENWOOD PRESS, PUBLISHERS
WESTPORT, CONNECTICUT

Library of Congress Cataloging in Publication Data

Varg, Paul A
Open door diplomat : the life of W. W. Rockhill.

Reprint of the ed. published by the University of Illinois Press, Urbana, which was issued as vol. 33, no. 4, of Illinois studies in the social sciences.
Bibliography: p.
Includes index.
1. Rockhill, William Woodville, 1854-1914.
2. United States--Foreign relations--20th century.
3. Eastern question (Far East) I. Title. II. Series: Illinois. University. Illinois studies in the social sciences ; v. 33, no. 4.
[E748.R674V37 1974] 327'.2'0924 [B] 74-20342

ISBN 0-8371-7858-4

Originally published in 1952 by the University of Illinois Press, Urbana

Reprinted with the permission of the University of Illinois Press

Reprinted in 1974 by Greenwood Press, a division of Williamhouse-Regency Inc.

Library of Congress Catalog Card Number 74-20342

ISBN 0-8371-7858-4

Printed in the United States of America

To

HELEN

Preface

William Woodville Rockhill made important contributions in the fields of diplomacy, exploration, and historical study. Diplomacy became his career, and his role in the formulation of American Far Eastern policy assures him a permanent place in the annals of the Republic. Even when his official duties were pressing, Rockhill remained an active scholar, and down to the closing days of his life he continued his fruitful research in Oriental studies. His Tibetan explorations in his earlier years earned him a reputation as an authority on the geography of that remote area and as a keen observer of its political and social customs. He was an intimate friend of Theodore Roosevelt, John Hay, and Henry Adams in the United States, a close acquaintance of such eminent Orientalists as Henri Cordier and Friedrich Hirth, and he knew well most of the statesmen serving the famous Empress Dowager of China. His diplomatic duties carried him to Peking, Seoul, Athens, St. Petersburg, and Constantinople.

The importance of W. W. Rockhill was first called to my attention by the late Professor Harley F. MacNair of the University of Chicago. Professor MacNair helped me in many ways with his pertinent suggestions as to lines of investigation. My colleagues at The Ohio State Unversity, Robert H. Bremner, William A. Williams, and Harry Coles, have given generously of their time and have made many helpful suggestions. Professor Foster Rhea Dulles has also generously shared with me his own first-hand knowledge of the Orient. Courtland Hoppin, grandson of W. W. Rockhill, has been most cooperative in giving me access to the Rockhill Papers. Miss Marion Crutch of Litchfield, Connecticut, a friend of the Rockhill family, provided papers of great importance which are in her possession. Mr. William Phillips very kindly granted me an interview and told me of some of his experiences while working with Rockhill. Miss Zara Powers, director of the manuscript room at the Sterling Memorial Library, Yale University, contributed through her assistance with the Rockhill Papers. I am also indebted to the members of the staffs at the National Archives and Library of Congress. My wife provided invaluable criticisms and encouragement and also performed the laborious chore of typing the manuscript.

PAUL A. VARG

The Ohio State University

Contents

CHAPTER ONE

Apprenticeship of a Diplomat

When Henry Adams had finished reading *Diary of A Journey through Mongolia and Tibet,* he wrote to the author, his good friend William Woodville Rockhill: "I feel quite a new spring of self-esteem that I should be able to treat you with familiarity. It is as though I had lived on intimate terms with Marco Polo, and had Genghis Khan for dinner." Adams scolded him for being overly modest in relating his story of adventure "as though it were a ramble in Pennsylvania Avenue" with Tibet "a kind of ornamental pleasure-ground somewhere near Georgetown." [1]

The editor of his publishing house had already pleaded with Rockhill to recount some of his hardships. To this Rockhill had replied that writing fifty pages of the dangers and hardships involved would make of him "a driveling idiot" and it was "really too humiliating for a man who has given a good many years of his life to the study of a country, even as remote a one as Central Asia, to find that the only thing that is of real interest to his fellow beings in all that he has done is of the most trivial character and absolutely of no interest to him." [2]

It was typical of this six-foot-four diplomat and scholar that he should be more concerned with the scientific facts concerning Tibet than with the dramatic hardships of a journey through the most desolate areas of the world. Having no appetite for public acclaim, Rockhill's impact on American foreign policy, scholarship, and geographical exploration has remained largely unrecognized to this day. Yet his refusal to pander to the public taste for dramatics did not prevent him from gaining the recognition of his peers.

Rockhill was one of a small group, including men of such catholic tastes as Theodore Roosevelt, Henry Adams, and Alfred Thayer Mahan, who, forty years before World War II, viewed the world as a community of nations wherein the United States must play the role of a full-grown citizen. Having spent most of his younger years outside of the United States, Rockhill was a cosmopolitan in a generation of provincials. After an education in France and three years with the French Foreign Legion in Algeria, he became a rancher on the cattleman's frontier in New Mexico, riding the range, throwing steers, and castrating calves. In the off-seasons he studied Chinese and Sanskrit. From the cow country

[1] *Letters of Henry Adams,* ed. Worthington Chauncey Ford (Boston: Houghton Mifflin Co., 1938), II, 63.

[2] W. W. Rockhill to H. E. Scudder, March 22, 1895, Rockhill Papers, Yale University. Unless otherwise noted, the Rockhill Papers cited hereafter are in the Yale collection.

Rockhill returned to France and spent two years studying ancient Buddhist scriptures. The next five years he resided in Peking, dividing his time between his duties as Secretary of the United States Legation and learning to speak Tibetan. In 1889 and again in 1891 he explored Mongolia and Tibet. Then followed important positions in Washington, including one year as Assistant Secretary of State under Grover Cleveland. With the election of McKinley, political exigencies sent him to Athens as Minister; in 1899 John Hay, recently appointed Secretary of State, arranged for his return to Washington. Later Rockhill represented his country in Peking, St. Petersburg, and Constantinople.

Although diplomacy became his career, Rockhill was essentially a scholar. While he was Secretary of Legation in Peking, his devotion to his studies so irritated the Minister, Charles Denby, that a bitter quarrel ensued and Rockhill was dismissed. Later, when Rockhill became Minister to China, although he maintained an office in the chancery of the Legation and wrote his own dispatches, his library was his workshop. Except for his afternoon walks on the wall at the edge of the city, he lived in his study with his Chinese manuscripts; he remained a scholar, and, therefore, an enigma to his staff. Whether Rockhill loved Tibetan studies more because he found pleasure in them or because they provided an escape from society, it would be futile for a biographer to assay.

Rockhill's motto was: "Love things, don't love people—things will give you pleasure." It was the maxim of a man who had little patience with human foibles. In St. Petersburg social life bored him; social events frequently caused him to comment in his diary, "Stupider, stupider, stupider!!!" This hatred was more than a dislike of the small talk of dull social events. His anti-social tendencies bordered on misanthropy. He was incapable of making a show of friendship, and he limited affection to his closest associates. To most of his acquaintances he seemed austere, self-sufficient. Few people penetrated beyond his reserve, and, if he let down the bars, it was likely to be in a moment of anger.

Alice Roosevelt, after visiting Rockhill in Peking, described him as "very tall and of an almost washed-out fairness," a man who had "grown to look curiously Chinese." She felt "that China had gotten into his blood; that if he let his mustache grow and pulled it down at the corners in a long twist, and wore Chinese clothes, he could have passed for a serene expounder" of Confucian philosophy.[3]

Among those on Rockhill's staff while he was Minister to China was William Phillips, later Assistant Secretary of State under Franklin Delano Roosevelt. Shortly after his arrival in the Chinese-Manchu capital, Phillips was stricken with typhoid and confined to a hospital. When he recovered, Mrs. Rockhill, whom he described as "a saint to me," invited him to stay at the Legation. To the Legation staff Rockhill seemed a kind of tyrant, a man whose only exercise was an afternoon walk with his wife, and a person of very few likes and many violent dis-

[3] Alice Roosevelt Longworth, *Crowded Hours: Reminiscences of Alice Roosevelt Longworth* (New York: Charles Scribner's Sons, 1933), p. 33.

likes. Years later Phillips recalled that Rockhill spent most of his time in the library—a library "shut-in," Phillips called him. What he was doing, none of his staff knew. But they did know about his periods of depression; they secretly referred to them as "mental gout."

The occasions when he was charming—and he could be charming—were few. Phillips once attended a Chinese luncheon given in the Minister's honor when, dressed in native costume and speaking Chinese fluently, Rockhill seemed to be genuinely enjoying himself. There is no better picture of Rockhill than that given by Phillips in a letter to his mother after his first few months in Peking. He wrote:

> Mr. Rockhill is a tremendously hard worker and has no pleasures outside of his work. He never rides, rarely dines out, and has no amusement whatsoever,—which is bad for any man. He is a difficult man to solve and difficult to get on with unless you are careful, and I never feel that if I stand well with him for the present it means much for the future. That is, he takes a violent fancy to a person and as quickly changes around to a dislike which he doesn't attempt to conceal. I have already seen several instances of this although fortunately the wind has blown in my favor so far. I admire Mrs. Rockhill very much and no one could have been nicer and kinder than she. No ordinary woman could have got on with Mr. Rockhill without difficulties and she has done it by sinking her own ideas and opinions entirely in his.
>
> On reading this it seems to convey the idea that I don't like my chief which is entirely erroneous. He is a splendid man to work with but it is socially that he is uncertain and of course we are all thrown together very intimately in this little community.[4]

To younger men embarking on diplomatic careers, Rockhill was known as the "Big Chief." Their lot was not an easy one; salaries were niggardly and the system of promotions placed little emphasis on meritorious work. The "Big Chief" was their champion who led the fight for an improved consular service and greater recognition of the importance to the country of a strong diplomatic corps. J. V. A. MacMurray, career diplomat, who worked with Rockhill during his early years in the foreign service, stated:

> He was not only one of the relatively few men of real professional competence to represent our country before the days of an organized American Foreign Service, but one of the few of that older generation who contributed, so to speak, to the spiritual working capital of the newly inaugurated Service by his recognition of the fact that the Chief must be no less loyal to his subordinates than he expects them to be to him.[5]

When William Woodville Rockhill was eleven years of age his family moved to France, and during all his life thereafter he resided in the United States for a total of only thirteen years. His constant moving about made him restless; he yearned for change no matter where fate placed him. After his first tour of duty

[4] Letter from William Phillips in Peking to his mother, August 27, 1905. This letter was read to the author by Mr. Phillips.

[5] J. V. A. MacMurray to author, November 14, 1946.

in China he resided in Washington, where he busied himself writing articles for magazines and seeking another position in the foreign service. He wrote to a friend: "I am also endeavoring to get another diplomatic appointment and I hear from the State Dept. that I am thought of for Korea. So be it, rather a cycle of Cathay or Korea than fifty years of America for me." [6] Although he yearned for his native land in later years and bemoaned the fact that he had been so long absent from it, it is doubtful that he ever understood it. An old friend once said that if Rockhill had been asked about the United States, he would probably have been "snippy."

His unconventional interests and inscrutable traits seem strange in view of his heritage. For more than two hundred years, Rockhills had labored in the American community as merchants, as doctors, and as tillers of the soil; they had held local political positions and had served in the military forces. The first member of the family to arrive on the North American continent was Edward Rockhill, who left Addingfleete in Yorkshire, England, in 1686 and settled near Mansfield Square, Chesterfield Township, New Jersey.

William Rockhill's grandfather, Thomas C. Rockhill, learned the trade of merchant while indentured to Silas Weir, of Philadelphia. The certificate of indenture, dated December 3, 1806, laid down what appear to a later generation as harsh terms. For a period of five years and twenty-four days Thomas was to "learn his art, trade and mystery," and in return was to serve his "master faithfully, his secrets keep, his lawful commands every where obey." [7]

Evidently the apprentice acquired the "art, trade and mystery" of his master, since in later years he became a highly successful merchant. His financial backing of Josiah Gregg, one of the early traders who carried goods over the Santa Fe Trail, led that enterprising merchant to dedicate a book on the overland trade with Mexico to Thomas C. Rockhill.[8] In later years, other Rockhills achieved prominence in foreign trade, among them a cousin of W. W. Rockhill whose firm represented some of the largest importers and exporters in Europe and the Orient.

When William was a child of ten months, his father, Thomas C. Rockhill, Jr., died. At the age of thirty-five, the father was entering a promising career as a lawyer in Philadelphia. A friend noted that he had attended St. Mary's College in Baltimore and that "a more honorable, refined, and accomplished Christian gentleman, he had never seen. His professional acquirements were of a high order; his knowledge of letters extensive, and his taste in them excellent."[9] The *Legal Intelligencer* of Philadelphia carried a long editorial lamenting the loss

[6] Rockhill to Alfred E. Hippisley, December 17, 1889, Rockhill Papers.

[7] Certificate of indenture of Thomas C. Rockhill, December 3, 1806, Rockhill Papers.

[8] Diary and letters of Josiah Gregg. *Southwestern Enterprises, 1840-1847,* ed. Maurice Garland Fulton (2 vols.; Norman: University of Oklahoma Press, 1941), I, 126-27.

[9] Newspaper clipping "Meeting of Philadelphia Bar—Death of Thomas C. Rockhill, Jr.," Rockhill Papers.

to the profession. The career of William Woodville Rockhill might have been radically different had his father lived. The death led to William's being taken to France. There it was that the youth acquired an interest in the Orient and an international outlook different from that of most Americans of the nineteenth century.

Rockhill's mother came from the Woodville family of Baltimore, Maryland. Left a widow when her younger son was less than a year old, it was she who bore the responsibility for his education and training. So clearly did William show the influence of his remarkable mother that he becomes less enigmatic only when the facts about this stormy, ambitious, intelligent woman are known.

Dorothea Anna Woodville had a distinguished ancestry. A great-grandfather, Samuel Ogle, succeeded Benedict Leonard Calvert in 1731 as the Proprietary Governor of Maryland. With the exception of two brief interludes, Samuel Ogle served as Governor until his death in 1752, enjoying a popular and successful administration. A son, Benjamin Ogle, grandfather of Dorothea Anna, held the same office for a brief term after the founding of the Republic.

In her maiden days Rockhill's mother knew only the festive side of America. There were visits to Belair, the ancestral estate west of Annapolis, with its deer park of six hundred acres, its race track, kennels, and bowling green, and the old mansion, the materials for which had been imported from England. There were also the gay social events in the nearby national capital where the vivacious, attractive, red-haired Dorothea danced with young naval officers. There were summers at Newport, the most fashionable resort on the coast; in the winter season, the Baltimore social calendar provided a continuous round of gaiety. Of the rise of factories and ugly red tenement houses in the river valleys of New England and the neighboring states, and of the new nation emerging in the Mississippi Valley, Dorothea Anna Woodville knew nothing; many of the great social and economic developments at the turn of the century were similarly to escape the notice of her illustrious son.

Yet, in spite of the frivolity of her early life, there emerged a woman whose vigor and determination enabled her granddaughter to write: "it was to her courage and determination; to her blind faith and blinder devotion; to her patent faults as well as her innumerable virtues that my father owed that early education and austere background that made him the astonishing combination that he was." [10]

When Dorothea married Thomas C. Rockhill, Jr., of Philadelphia, she shut the door to the carefree life of her early years. She bore her first son in 1852, and gave birth to William on April 1, 1853. When her husband died of tuberculosis the following year, leaving her with an annuity of twelve hundred dollars, there was no choice but to accept the invitation of her mother-in-law to move to the old Rockhill residence on Pine Street. For all its spaciousness, the house was

[10] An account of her father's early life written by Dorothy Rockhill in 1925. The manuscript was loaned to the author by Courtland Hoppin, grandson of W. W. Rockhill.

not large enough to accommodate two such vigorous spirits as the young widow and the old Mrs. Rockhill. The mother-in-law, in the eyes of a descendant, was tyrannical and cantankerous while the young Mrs. Rockhill was independent, intolerant, and rebellious. Holding the purse-strings, the mother-in-law was free to dominate; and, according to the younger woman, the domination took the form of directing the lives of the two small boys, giving them sweets to their hearts' content, encouraging them to be disobedient to their mother, and isolating them from the benefits of an education. The battle of the sons lasted for nine long years and then ended with the mother making a victorious retreat to France. Whoever was at fault for the strife on Pine Street the fact remains that, at the age of ten, William Woodville Rockhill could neither read nor write.

Rockhill grew to manhood in France knowing few of the normal pleasures of adolescence. The young widow and her two sons settled in a little apartment on or near the Place Pereire, and in due course the boys entered the Lycée Condorcet. In a strange land, and with money sufficient only for the barest necessities, the family of three lived a simple and austere life. Only in the mother's determination to have her sons acquire the best in learning were the Rockhill boys favored, and her determination soon became their own. In spite of the difficulty of having to use a foreign tongue, William did remarkably well and acquired the important habit of success. When he entered the École Impérial Centrale des Arts et Manufactures, he ranked ninth among two hundred candidates. It seems reasonable to believe that these years made him what he was—a kind of driving perfectionist, a zealous scholar escaping from the world, a man incapable of personal warmth.

News from the United States was as rare as it was precious, but occasionally a friend or a friend's friend traveling through Paris called on the Rockhills. Among these visitors were Marie Louise Tyson and her daughter Caroline who had come to France to reside after Mr. Tyson's death. Young William, aged thirteen, fell in love with Caroline, aged twelve. The visit was to have more than casual consequences.

Yet the boy's falling in love at thirteen was probably one of the few occasions when he gave way to the lighter and more normal life of an adolescent. The schools which young Rockhill attended called for long hours of work, and he had the added disadvantages of a late start and of learning a foreign tongue. After one year at the École des Arts et Manufactures where he took courses in calculus, mechanics, geometry, physics, chemistry, geology, and architecture, there was a short respite in 1871 in southern France, near Bordeaux. The older boy, Thomas, always frail, was in bad health, and Mrs. Rockhill believed that a change in climate would be beneficial. The trip not only saved them from being caught in Paris when the victorious Germans laid siege to the city, but it resulted in Mrs. Rockhill's conversion to Catholicism and her introduction to Monsieur Greppin, a Swiss, whom she was to marry.

The stay in southern France was brief. As soon as the health of Thomas and conditions in Paris permitted, Mrs. Rockhill brought the boys back to Paris where they continued the all-important business of getting an education. Through the assistance of the American Minister to France, William gained admission to St. Cyr, the French equivalent of West Point. Whether the recent Franco-Prussian War had stimulated his interest in military affairs, or whether the decision was dictated by the necessity of choosing a career—he was now eighteen—the records fail to reveal. In any event, in later years he showed no interest in military life. He was always a man of thought rather than a man of action. Nevertheless, he went to St. Cyr where he distinguished himself as a student.

In 1872 Mrs. Rockhill married Monsieur Greppin, much to the displeasure of her son William. Only occasionally did she see her boys. In 1874, shortly after graduating from the École Polytechnique, Thomas died of tuberculosis. The mother lived to be ninety: she died in 1913. To the end she possessed vigor and vitality in spite of blindness and a lonely life in a Swiss village. The American Consul entered the following in the Miscellaneous Record Book of the consulate:

> She was a fine example of the gentlewoman of the old school, intelligent, warm-hearted, simple in tastes, knowing the gentle art of growing old gracefully. In spite of her great age, she was youthful in mind and heart. She combined both strength and gentleness in her high character. She lived a life of purest piety in the faith to which she was devoted, but was broadminded in her religious tolerance.[11]

Apparently it was while a student at St. Cyr that William Rockhill's interests took a new turn. Ernest Renan, philologist and historian who had been ousted in 1862 because of unorthodox views, returned to the Collège de France in 1871. Renan was a student of Semitic languages. Rockhill became an admirer of the scholar, and it was from Renan that he acquired an interest in non-Aryan languages which appears to have been the stepping stone to his interest in the Orient. He also became acquainted with Abbé Huc's book, *Souvenirs d'un voyage dans la Tartarie,* which gave him the idea of exploring Tibet. His spare hours were spent at the Bibliothèque Nationale where he studied Tibetan under Leon Peer, a student of the Far East. Foregoing the usual pleasures of student life, Rockhill worked fourteen hours a day on his linguistic studies and his regular courses. He graduated from St. Cyr with honors in 1873.

Upon his graduation Rockhill joined the Foreign Legion and served as a sub-lieutenant in the province of Oran in Algeria until 1876. In that year he resigned his commission and returned to the United States for the first time. He kissed ladies' hands, wore a monocle, and cursed shoe cleaners because they didn't polish the soles of his shoes as well as the tops. In short, Rockhill had acquired the manners and attitudes of a nineteenth-century French officer and was a stranger in the land of his birth. According to family reminiscence he spoke English with a foreign accent, and his letters were literal translations from the French.

[11] Copy of an entry in the Miscellaneous Record Book of the American consulate, Geneva, Switzerland, Rockhill Papers.

Rockhill had not seen Caroline Tyson since she had left Paris six years earlier, but he had never given up the idea of marrying her. Apparently Caroline had given him little encouragement, but he had continued to write to her and to besiege a mutual acquaintance with inquiries. On his arrival in the United States he found that Caroline was at White Sulpher Springs, West Virginia, and he went there only to find—after his several thousands of miles' pilgrimage—that Caroline was all but engaged. Whether Caroline was won by the audacity of his trip or intrigued by his foreign manners remains unknown, but, before the month of August was over, Rockhill and Caroline Tyson were engaged. On December 14, 1876, only four months later, they were married. She was the second woman to enter his life, and, like his mother, she became his support and gave him the only friendship he craved.

After a honeymoon in France and Switzerland, the newly married Rockhills returned to Glenelg, Mrs. Tyson's estate in Maryland. Mr. Tyson, who had died when Caroline was five years old, had entered into speculative business ventures and had acquired a small fortune temporarily. The family finances were in a precarious state when he died, but his wife had retained Glenelg until after the Civil War when she sold the estate and moved to Paris. In 1870 the purchasers were unable to meet the payments, and Mrs. Tyson resumed possession. Not long after Rockhill and his bride came to Glenelg in 1877, it became necessary to sell once again.

On the last day of the year another event of importance occurred—the birth of a daughter, Dorothy. Facing new family responsibilities and having limited financial resources, Rockhill had to find some means of livelihood.

His choice of occupation was not long delayed however, and, for a graduate of St. Cyr and a scholar, the choice was most remarkable. Leh Cooper, an uncle of Mrs. Rockhill's, had gone west for a visit and returned with reports of the great profits to be made in the booming cattle industry. The wild herds of Texas longhorns were being driven from Texas and neighboring territories to the outlying points of the newly constructed railroads in Kansas. At the cowtowns of Abilene and Dodge City the cattleman sold his stock at a price netting fancy profits. Cooper's reports suggested a way out for the young man weighted with family responsibilities. The settled society of the older seaboard states offered few opportunities to a man who was without a profession or special training. Rockhill joined Cooper in the purchase of land and cattle in the frontier territory of New Mexico.

In January, Leh Cooper and Rockhill, now twenty-four years old, set out for the scene of operations. Some three months later the ladies followed—Mrs. Rockhill; Dorothy, aged three months; Mrs. Tyson; and Cooper's six-year-old daughter. Rockhill met them at Trinidad, Colorado, the nearest railway terminus, and then took them the rest of the way by wagon. At the end of the trail was the Rockhill ranch consisting of a small wooden shanty, a chicken house, and one or two shacks. Mrs. Rockhill appropriately dubbed it "Poverty Flat." Mrs. Tyson and Cooper's daughter soon made a retreat to civilization, leaving the Rockhills and Uncle Leh to cope with the loneliness of the great plains.

Rockhill tackled his new tasks with the same vigor he had displayed as a student. At round-up time he proved his worth by throwing steers for branding. While he and Uncle Leh were away at the round-up, the attractive and cheerful Mrs. Rockhill was left alone with the baby and Minnie, a servant girl, remembered chiefly as the one seated when all others remained standing for the taking of a photograph. There were off-seasons when the demands upon the rancher diminished, and during those weeks Rockhill isolated himself to study Chinese and Sanskrit. It was well understood that he was not to be disturbed, and weeks would pass when he hardly spoke. But on one occasion he spoke too much. On his way to town a talkative stranger on the stagecoach queried him about the country. Rockhill showed considerable feeling in reporting that there had been a good deal of trouble about "that scoundrel Elkins, who had been land-grabbing again." Of course, the stranger was none other than Stephen B. Elkins, later United States Senator.

Rockhill at one time thought he had discovered a sulphur spring on his ranch. When a dead donkey was found at the bottom of the well, nothing more was said about it outside of the family.

In 1881 the ranch was sold without loss of capital. Still handicapped by limited financial resources, Rockhill and his family went to Montreux, Switzerland, where Rockhill's mother (now Mrs. Greppin) was residing. During the next three years the ex-rancher established his reputation as a Tibetan scholar. In 1883 his first book, *Udonvarga,* a translation of the northern Buddhist version of *Dhammapada,* appeared. The book contained moral and prudential maxims on such subjects as instability, cupidity, affection, chastity, pain, and piety. In the course of the next year two more books came from his pen, *The Life of Buddha,* derived from Tibetan sources, and *Pratimoksha sutra,* a French translation from Tibetan of a part of the Buddhist scriptures. A number of English scholars wrote letters of congratulation and W. D. Whitney, a leading American Orientalist, expressed pleasure at Rockhill's work. A missionary in Mongolia wrote enthusiastically—and urged Rockhill to give his heart to Christ and his life to his suffering fellow man.

For Rockhill's family, Montreux was hardly more pleasant than the ranch in New Mexico. Working intently at his studies in the small apartment, Rockhill would tolerate no noise; little Dorothy's earliest recollection was an admonition to keep quiet. When he lost his temper—and he could break into a rage never to be forgotten by his victims—his red moustache would droop at both ends, "until he could (and did) bite the ends while he stared off into space, wrapped in gloom and silence." Dorothy recalled:

> These were the moments in which to disappear or, when that was impossible, to make oneself as small, silent and inconspicuous as one could; not, indeed, that one was ever encouraged as a child to be anything else. Army discipline had made of

him something of a drill sergeant. We seldom met, in those days, except at lunch, and communion between us was limited on his part to "sit up," "take your elbows off the table," "stop playing with the salt." And yet there were times when he would emerge from weeks of moodiness into a riot of gay spirits, when he was boyish, delightful and absurd.[12]

Among the few amusing incidents of Dorothy's early life were her father's attempts at singing—the one song he knew was "Voici le sabre de mon père"—which always brought tears streaming down his cheeks. His endeavor to memorize poetry provided occasions for humor, too, for, despite an extraordinary memory, his greatest achievement was the first two lines of a poem by Poe.

The three years at Montreux were marked by real poverty. Then suddenly, and wholly unexpectedly, Mrs. Rockhill inherited between sixty and seventy thousand dollars from a cousin. To a family bordering on penury it was a fortune. Dorothy recalled: "We moved from our little flat to the Hotel National. I remember it as a palace. We got new clothes, and my father set about realising his dream of getting to China."

[12] Manuscript on the early life of her father, by Dorothy Rockhill.

CHAPTER TWO

An American in Mongolia and Tibet

The newly acquired fortune became an endowment for the continuation of Rockhill's Tibetan studies and for the exploration of inner Asia. Since his first introduction to Oriental studies, Rockhill had wished to go to China. In the summer of 1883 he made inquiries regarding the possibility of an appointment as Military Attaché. His aim was to get to Peking where he could study Chinese and learn the spoken language of Tibet, a necessary tool before he could hope to explore the country.

In April, 1884, he received an appointment as Second Secretary of Legation in Peking. The Rockhills left for America in June, and two months later they embarked on their first trip to the Orient. At the time of his appointment the position carried no pay, but in July of the same year Congress passed a bill providing a salary of $1,800. A year later he was promoted to Secretary of Legation at a stipend of $2,625.

Having arrived in Peking, Rockhill had some difficulty in finding a teacher of Tibetan; no foreigner could help him and natives were suspicious of the use he might make of his acquisition. Finally he secured the services of a lama from Lhasa, and during the next four years—at the same time he was studying Chinese—he learned to speak Tibetan. The lama and Rockhill became warm friends. Once the lama told him that in Tibet he would be considered a very handsome man. Rockhill was pleased until the lama added, that in his country very large noses and ears were admired, and Rockhill's were enormous.

These first years in China were happy ones. Rockhill found enough work to satisfy him. As Secretary of Legation he acquired first-hand information about diplomatic affairs. He kept a file of all communications, transcribed the letters of the Minister, and prepared visas for American citizens.

In November, 1886, Rockhill went to Korea on temporary duty as Chargé d'Affaires to aid Ensign George C. Foulk. Korea was a hotbed of intrigue between Chinese, Japanese, and Russians. The Koreans, led by a weak king, were wholly incapable of fending for themselves. The position of the United States in Korea was a delicate one. A group of missionaries led by Horace Allen, a medical doctor representing the Presbyterians, caused a critical situation by their zeal in evangelizing, although a national law of Korea barred their activities.[1] Rockhill had written earlier to the Department of State of "a restless disposition on the

[1] Fred Harvey Harrington, in his scholarly and delightful biography of Horace Allen, *God, Mammon and the Japanese* (Madison: University of Wisconsin Press, 1944), tells the story of the intrigue at Seoul.

part of the missionaries in Corea to exceed the bounds of prudence in the prosecution of evangelical work." [2] Yet, Rockhill was friendly to Allen and did what he could to help the missionaries. He also did what he could for business interests; when a merchant named Townshend was threatened with eviction, Rockhill called for the protection of a naval vessel.[3] During his brief stay at Seoul in the winter of 1886-1887, he first saw the swirl of the winds of clashing imperialisms. He later wrote: "Korea is the place . . . there you will see diplomacy in the raw; diplomacy without gloves, perfume or phrases."

No one could have pursued his studies with a greater singleness of purpose than Rockhill, but in Peking he had to break away from his chosen work and participate in the social life of the small group of foreigners. While he continued to work diligently during the day, he and Mrs. Rockhill attended the evening parties given by the foreign representatives. However, he discovered a few people among them whom he enjoyed. Sir Nicholas O'Connor, later British Ambassador to Turkey; Sir Edward Goschen, British Ambassador to Germany when war broke out in 1914; and Baron von Kettler, later German Minister to China and killed by the Boxers, became his lifelong friends.

Times of trial and tribulation came also. Shortly after Rockhill's return from Korea in the spring of 1887, Dorothy was taken ill with smallpox and had to be sent to a hospital outside of Peking. Mrs. Rockhill, who was expecting a second child, could not accompany her. Rockhill hesitated to leave his wife to go with the sick child, but Mrs. Rockhill persuaded him. At the hospital he spent days and nights caring for Dorothy, giving himself unsparingly, until he, too, was taken ill. In Peking, Mrs. Rockhill had difficulty in getting a doctor because of her exposure to the dreaded smallpox. An English physician came to the rescue, and the wife of an English photographer attended her. When the second daughter, Margarita, was born, it was Baron von Kettler who stole out to the isolated hospital at night to deliver the good news to the father.

Rockhill did not lose sight of his original aim in seeking a position in China. Tibetan exploration was his goal, and, in 1886, he tried to obtain a leave from Minister Charles Denby. Denby, woefully uninformed, replied: "If you're so anxious to go, I'll try to get you appointed Minister there." [4] Of course, Tibet was under the sovereignty of China and had no diplomatic relations with outside countries except through Peking. When Denby still refused to grant him a leave of absence, Rockhill sought the aid of James Wilson, who had recently returned to the United States after working on the negotiation of a railroad contract in China. Wilson promised to talk to Secretary of State Thomas F. Bayard and to an influential senator "about the glory to be gained by the State Depart-

[2] W. W. Rockhill to Secretary of State T. F. Bayard, February 5, 1885, cited by Harrington, *op. cit.*, pp. 98-99.

[3] *Ibid.*, February 10, 1887, pp. 128-29.

[4] Manuscript on the early life of her father, by Dorothy Rockhill.

ment by your success in doing what everybody has failed to carry through."[5] But Wilson's efforts proved futile and the trip to Tibet had to be postponed.

Relations with Denby appear to have been the one unpleasant feature of life in Peking. The Minister knew neither French nor any other foreign language while Rockhill, his subordinate, spoke French fluently and had a good command of Chinese. Nor did Denby's knowledge of geography gain him the respect of his staff—he spoke of "Hungaria," and thought that Cossacks came from Corsica. These gaps were not compensated by humility as far as the members of the Legation could discern. The Minister was ever ready to assert his full authority. Even Denby's youngest son reminded Dorothy: "Your father's like a kind of servant to my father. He has to obey him, no matter what he tells him to do." Never one to bow easily, Rockhill pursued an independent course, defending what he considered to be his rights with characteristic stubbornness. He pursued his Tibetan studies until Denby complained that he neglected his official duties.

When Rockhill returned to the United States on leave in the summer of 1888, his career in the foreign service came to an abrupt—but only temporary—halt. After a friendly interview with Secretary of State Bayard, Rockhill went to Sea Girt, New Jersey. In a few days he received a letter from the Secretary stating that he had not had opportunity to discuss the matter of relations between Colonel Denby and Rockhill. The Minister had written letters complaining of Rockhill's lack of cooperation. On July 5, Rockhill wrote a long letter to Bayard tendering his resignation and answering the charges made by Denby.[6] The controversy appears to have been largely a case of conflicting personalities. Bayard refused to become a party to either side, and took the position that the strained relations would cause the public interest to suffer.[7] Upon Rockhill's resignation, Denby's son became Secretary of Legation.

The break with Denby and his consequent resignation as Secretary of Legation left Rockhill free to enter upon his long projected trip of Tibetan exploration, and he left for China early in the autumn of 1888. His object was to secure information of a historical, geographical, and ethnographical nature. Having depended on personal financial resources, Rockhill's equipment was more like that of a geographer setting out on a week-end field trip than that of an explorer on a long and dangerous journey. He noted with satisfaction: "My outfit was simple and inexpensive, for dressing and living like a Chinaman, I was incumbered neither with clothes nor foreign stores, bedding, tubs, medicines, nor any of the other endless impedimenta which so many travelers consider absolute necessities." [8] With one Chinese servant, Rockhill set out from

[5] James Wilson to Rockhill, December 31, 1886, Rockhill Papers.

[6] Rockhill to Bayard, July 5, 1888, Rockhill Papers.

[7] Bayard to Rockhill, July 7, 1888, Rockhill Papers.

[8] W. W. Rockhill, *The Land of the Lamas: Notes of A Journey through China, Mongolia, and Tibet* (New York: Century Co., 1891), p. 2.

Peking early on the morning of December 17, 1888. In eight months he traveled 4,900 miles over frozen deserts and mountain ranges 16,000 feet in altitude.

Northern China, with its drab villages of tumble-down houses, small shops, and narrow streets where many dogs and lank pigs roamed, offered little of interest except the great Buddhist sanctuary of Wu-t'ai shan in the province of Shansi. Set in a valley, the sixty-five temples with bright tiled roofs and golden spires made a fitting shrine for the tens of thousands of Mongols and Tibetans who went there on pilgrimages each year. Inside the temples, images of gold, silver, bronze, and clay gods greeted the devout with kind or angry mien. Before the deities, offerings of fruit, confectionery, and bowls of clear water placed by the faithful gave testimony to the piety of the Mongol peasants and nomads. Innumerable little brass lamps, filled with butter and arranged in rows before the altars, cast a hallowed light.

On February 6, Rockhill reached the town of Hsi-ning Fu and experienced his first encounter with suspicious officials. Told to report to the authorities the next day to explain the purpose of his trip, he changed his Chinese gown for a big red cloth like that worn by Mongol lamas and left the village early in the morning with a party of K'alk'a Mongols.

From Hsi-ning Fu he went to the Lamasery of Kumbum where a religious festival had attracted hundreds of people from the hills. The streets were gay and full of life. On one of the hillsides a fair was in progress. There were open-air restaurants, butchers' and bakers' stalls, dealers in hides and pelts, peepshows with obscene pictures of European origin, gambling tables, and traders with a variety of trinkets. Business was thriving, especially the peepshows and gambling tables, when the crowd suddenly scattered. A lama censor accompanied by six or eight lamas with black stripes across their foreheads and around their arms entered and with their heavy whips struck at all unfortunate enough to be within reach. Rockhill, greatly amused, followed the censor and "saw the peep-show knocked down, Punch and Judy laid mangled beside it, the owners whipped and put to flight, and the majesty of ecclesiastical law and morality duly vindicated."

The religious festival which occasioned the activity at Kumbum also provided an exhibition of butter bas-reliefs. The two principal pieces of sculpture were each about ten feet high and twenty feet long. Rows of little butter lamps illuminated the brightly colored portrayals of various heavenly abodes and the different hells. The hundreds of little figures each carefully worked out testified to the pride that the sculptors took in their work.

Rockhill had a special interest in the Kumbum Lamasery as it was here that modern Lamaism was born. The Lamasery was founded by Tsongk'apa, a preacher and reformer of the late fourteenth and early fifteenth centuries, who established the branch of Buddhism known as the Yellow Church, the one which still prevails in Tibet and Mongolia. Upon his death, Tsongk'apa transmigrated into the person of Gedun drumpa, the first of a series of incarnated gods known as *Panch'en rinpoche.* These divine personages acquired the title *jya-ts'o.* Translated into the language of the Mongols, *jya-ts'o* became Dalai Lama. Later the Dalai Lama became the political ruler of Tibet.

By May, Rockhill had reached eastern Tibet where, in a distance of about six hundred miles, he passed thirty-six lamaseries. In a population estimated at 150,000, approximately one-fifth were lamas. They lived in the lowlands in monasteries resembling fortresses, and while ostensibly devoted to the pious life of monks, the lamas seemed to Rockhill to combine with their holiness the qualities of unruly soldiers and traders. Well-armed and well-mounted, they frequently engaged in battles with their brethren of rival lamaseries.

Rockhill observed that there were three classes of lamas. At the top of the social pyramid were the officials charged with temporal and ceremonial duties, including a strict code of discipline which gave them the power of life and death over their brothers. Among this class were the forty-eight living saints who resided in various of the larger lamaseries. These were distinguished by their superior sanctity and devoted themselves to prayers and to fortune telling. Next in rank were the Gelong lamas, who had studied the sacred books and who had committed themselves to chastity, poverty, and to abstinence from tobacco, liquor, and other worldly pleasures. It was from this class that the officials were chosen. Lowest in rank were the Draba lamas who did the manual work. They had shaved their heads, taken the five minor vows, put on the red gown, and taken up residence in a lamasery. Only the Draba lamas were free to marry.

The wasted and forsaken upland areas of eastern Tibet offered a sad contrast to the richer valleys. Sand, gravel, occasional stiff grass, and stagnant pools repelled animals and humans alike. The high altitude, 14,500 feet, tested Rockhill's endurance as well as that of his horses and dogs who limped dejectedly behind. The snow squalls drenched the clothing of the men and the rare atmosphere nauseated them.

Rockhill found that Tibetans outside of the lamaseries lived in black tents having only two poles. Fireplaces of stone and mud were their only items of furniture. The Tibetan diet, wholly compatible with the general wretchedness, consisted of a brown dough made of tea, *tsamba* (barley flour), and butter, which usually was rancid. The whole sodden mass was washed down with tea.

Only in their forms of greeting one another did these nomads betray any taste for ceremony. In one area they held out both hands, palms uppermost, and stuck out their tongues; Lhasa men added to this by pulling their right ears and rubbing their left hips.

Rockhill noted that, with the exception of the extreme northern and northeastern portions of Tibet, the people were essentially of one race. The purest specimens were the Drupa or pastoral tribes. They averaged five feet five inches in height, had brachycephalic heads, wavy hair, high cheekbones, narrow noses with broad nostrils, and very thin beards. The women were stouter than the men, and their muscles were more fully developed since they did most of the heavy work.

The custom of never washing the body and the lack of cleanliness among the people filled Rockhill with dismay. Vermin were common, especially among the women, and it was not unusual to see them searching one another's hair. Rockhill wrote that "all captures belong to the original owner, who eats them with a relish, saying 'As they live on me, they can not be unclean food for me, though they might be for anyone else.' "

Rockhill kept voluminous and detailed notes. His published account contains detailed descriptions of the political organizations of the natives and of their mores, means of livelihood, and religious beliefs, as well as of their dwellings and utensils. The Tibetan lamaseries interested him greatly; he lived in various ones for several weeks. In the Kuo-mang ssu Lamasery he met Bu Lama, who, during his earlier days at the Peking Legation, had taught him to speak Tibetan. The ceremonies of the lamas and their manner of life were viewed by Rockhill in a truly objective manner and he never gave himself to either praise or criticism. He also collected facts of geography and animal life with great care.

On his return to the United States, he wrote numerous articles and a book entitled *The Land of the Lamas.* His writings are devoted to what he saw rather than to what he experienced. Students of ethnography, geography, and history found his reports of interest but those looking for a story of adventure were, for the most part, sadly disappointed. Rockhill made almost no reference to hardships encountered or to narrow escapes.

After spending 1890 and most of 1891 in writing his book and a series of articles for *Century Magazine,* Rockhill set forth on his second trip to Central Asia. His aim now was to traverse Tibet from northeast to southwest, leaving China from Kansu province and crossing Tibet into India. On December 1, 1891, Rockhill and his Chinese servant left Peking, this time in two hired carts. Not until the end of the following October did he return to the China coast.

During the intervening months he saw almost no members of his own race except a few missionaries stationed at the outposts of civilization. Rockhill showed considerable sympathy with Buddhism, and questioned the wisdom of trying to supplant it with Western Christianity. The Chinese and Mongols were opportunists and would readily affiliate themselves during a famine with a missionary station where food was to be had, but would as readily desert when the danger of starvation had passed. As to the relative merits of Catholic and Protestant missionaries, he thought better of the Catholic though he himself was a Protestant. He found the Catholics of more genial spirit and counted them among his best friends. He noted in his diary:

I reached Hsing-ch'eng at 7:30 P.M., and got a warm reception from Father von Belle and a Friday's meal—cold tea, dry bread and lard, used in place of butter. This is the usual style of living among Catholic missionaries. Among the Protestants, Crossette and James Gilmour tried it and consequently both were looked upon as "cranks" by their brethren, the former especially who lived for years an ideal Christian life, having no cares for the morrow, providing himself with neither raiment nor food and giving all to the poor.[9]

More characteristic than either praise or censure was Rockhill's extremely objective point of view, which later caused some missionaries to protest against his appointment as Minister to China.

During the greater part of his trip his only companions were the five men, Tibetans and Mongols, whom he had employed upon reaching Mongolia. The cook proved the only troublesome one in the lot. He stole food rations and appropriated Rockhill's clothes on one occasion. He was retained only because he was almost as indispensable as the compass. The guide, "a queer specimen of the Panaka Tibetan; a little, wizzened-up fellow of about fifty, with shaven head and no beard, a piercing eye and spare but well-muscled body," resorted to divination and primitive magic when the party became lost. Though these Asiatics offered little companionship, they served Rockhill reasonably well, and on occasion proved entertaining as well as useful. Rockhill wrote: "Last night Damba amused us by singing songs in Chinese, Lh'asan, Panaka and Mongol styles. He took off the Chinese admirably and I laughed until the tears ran down my cheeks—a rare treat (not the tears but the laugh) ; I have not had such a one for the last six months." [10]

Exploring Mongolia and Tibet provided few occasions for joviality. On the average the party covered more than twenty miles a day, traversing regions of loess where both the men and mules sank to their knees with each step. The glaring snow of the mountain ranges blinded them and daily rain and hail and strong winds cut their cheeks until they bled. During the part of the trip which Rockhill described as geographically important, they crossed sixty-nine passes, all of them rising over 14,500 feet above sea level. On one occasion, Rockhill almost lost his life while fording a stream.

We crossed the Yogore about two miles east of Kawa obo. The men in single file rode their ponies across the ice without accident, though it cracked ominously. As I started to cross Dowe shouted out, "Sems chung, sems chung, Ponbo-la!" ("Look out, look out, Sir!") but too late; the ice gave way under my horse and we both disappeared in the water, which was very deep and swift and about a foot or so below the lower surface of the ice. My baggy ch'uba and trousers held me up and I caught on to the ice where I was able to cling, though the current threw my legs against the ice with such violence that I could not draw myself out, but the pony was swept under. I shouted to the men to throw themselves flat on the ice and creep out to me, which they did, and after much trouble got me out, none the worse for the ducking.[11]

Infinitely more serious than the discomforts of traveling, including the filth,

[9] W. W. Rockhill, *Diary of A Journey through Mongolia and Tibet in 1891 and 1892* (Washington: Smithsonian Institution, 1894), p. 61.

[10] *Ibid.*, p. 168.

[11] *Ibid.*, p. 145.

was the danger of starvation. Though Rockhill had taken every precaution to guard against running out of food—buying as much as was available and as the pack animals could carry—the supplies ran low. The country on the Shire nor was bleak; the famished pack animals could not find so much as a tuft of grass on which to nibble. The men ate ass-flesh, but Rockhill prized cleanliness too much to join in eating the horrible mess they prepared. He was shocked at the quantity of filth they could eat—"hair, dung, blood, all goes, the scum on the boiling pot they hold to be a delicacy. . . ."

Daily rations had to be severely limited. Rockhill recorded in his diary the tenseness which grips starving men when in sight of game.

> Towards dark we saw a bull yak feeding on the hills west of our camp and we all turned out to get a shot at him. He started off at a great pace when we were half a mile off, and though we followed him until dark up and down hills we never got near enough to shoot. When one has been very hungry for over a month, stalking is exciting work. There is not even a sheldrake to be seen, not a lark nor a marmot; the silence of this vast wilderness is positively oppressive.[12]

And the following day he recorded that there was "absolutely nothing left to eat but a little flour and tea." The last cupful of *tsamba* was divided among the men a few days later. He had nothing left for himself but a small flask of brandy "which I have treasured up so far in case of an emergency, satisfying my desire for it with an occasional smell of the liquor." Early in July when all supplies were gone, Rockhill shot a wild ass:

> it fell at the first shot; we all ran up excitedly but the famished dogs were there before us, and up jumped the ass and made off. Do what I would I could not put my pony into even a trot; he was like his master, too played out for sport. The men took our misfortune with true Mohammedan stoicism; *Tien ming,* "it is Heaven's decree," was all they said, and mounting their ponies rode on.[13]

Late in July the exhausted party stumbled upon some nomads who were well supplied with food. Rockhill noted with glee that he and his men were revelling among the fleshpots of Tibet. But the encounter also meant the disruption of his plan to cross west of Tengri nor and enter India. The Tibetans, carrying out the orders of the authorities at Lhasa, prescribed a new route. Rockhill noted:

> I agreed finally to this; it will take me through unexplored country. It does not make much difference after all which way I go, though it is very disappointing not to be able to carry out my original plan—but who ever does in life? I am not twenty miles from the Tengri nor . . . I am ten days from Shigatse and not more than twenty-five from British India and six or seven weeks from home, but it will be four or five months before I reach there now by the long route I shall have to travel. *T'ien ming,* "it is Heaven's decree." [14]

---

[12] *Ibid.,* p. 221.

[13] *Ibid.,* p. 225.

[14] *Ibid.,* p. 238.

Far away in Berkeley, West Virginia, Mrs. Rockhill, without word for several months, had given him up for lost. His mother, equally desperate with anxiety, vowed to the Virgin that she would make a pilgrimage every summer to the shrine at Einsiedln, "and for further mortification travel third class, if She would bring him back safely," a vow which she kept until death. A garbled telegram from Shanghai arrived in Berkeley in October. A messenger asked that Mrs. Rockhill come to the office to help in deciphering the telegram. Certain that this could only be the final verification of her husband's death, her courage failed and she told the messenger that she would wait until the telegram could be re-transmitted. But the tenseness was too great, and Dorothy was sent to get the message. Eager for news of her father, Dorothy ran through the streets of the village to the telegraph office. The retransmitted message read: "Arrived Shanghai." That was enough; and she turned to run home. Mrs. Rockhill met her a few yards away, conscious-smitten that she had sent Dorothy off alone to bear the shock.

Weeks passed with no further word than that he was sailing and later a telegram stating when he would arrive at Hancock, the nearest railway station. On the appointed day Mrs. Rockhill and Dorothy were there to meet him. Dorothy wrote later:

> My mother had tortured herself with imagining all the things he had gone through, but the reality was worse than she had pictured. He was emaciated and almost blind from the months spent in the snow, and it frightened one to see the condition in which his nerves were after his many hardships. He could hardly speak when he met us, and all the way in the train he sat quite still holding my mother's hand with the tears rolling down his cheeks. Instead of a joyful reunion, we must have suggested partakers in some direful tragedy.[15]

[15] Manuscript on the early life of her father, by Dorothy Rockhill.

CHAPTER THREE

Adventures in Diplomacy

The hazards of exploration gave way to the uncertainties of a diplomatic career in 1893 when Rockhill accepted an appointment as Chief Clerk of the Department of State. The United States had yet to emerge from the sheltering chrysalis of nineteenth-century isolation, but the outside world beckoned with opportunities and challenged the Republic to greater consideration of its own security. Among Rockhill's friends in Washington—John Hay, Henry Cabot Lodge, Theodore Roosevelt, and Henry Adams—the doctrine of isolationism no longer evoked a feeling of piety. In the next two decades, partly as a result of Rockhill's influence, the United States was to venture forth as a full-scale protagonist in international affairs.

The Cleveland administration placed great value on Rockhill's services; after one year he was promoted to Third Assistant Secretary, and, on February 11, 1896, to Assistant Secretary of State. The *New York Tribune,* praising the appointment, stated that Rockhill would have charge of the consular service and relations with the Asiatic countries.

Among the letters of congratulation was one from Theodore Roosevelt, and it was not altogether reassuring.

> Three cheers! But where does this leave me as a Republican? When it was Gresham & Quincey, though I felt ashamed as an American, I didn't mind as a party man; but now when I *have* to be proud of Olney and yourself, I would like to know what are to become of my party principles?
>
> All I mind is that I fear this may be a less permanent position, and I never wish to see you leave the State Department until you go to China as minister.[1]

While Rockhill's interest was primarily in the Far East, Latin American affairs were of paramount importance at this particular time and he gave some of his attention to them. Relations with Great Britain became tense when President Cleveland called for arbitration of the boundary dispute between Great Britain and Venezuela. Rockhill defended the action of the United States in a letter to a British acquaintance who was in Peking.

> Don't worry about the Venezuela business and don't let any ill-feeling grow up between you and any Americans on that score. We have the same ideas as you about fair play, and we thought you were trying to strike Venezuela below the belt, accidentally it may be but still this called for a remark from us. The whole thing will have a very good effect on both sides of the Atlantic.
>
> Asiatic politics are, to my mind, a much more important factor in the world's

[1] Theodore Roosevelt to W. W. Rockhill, February 12, 1896, Rockhill Papers.

present history than American ones. You are getting everything over there in a grand old tangle and when you finally break loose and clear up the wreck, you will find that Russia is ahead, or I am very much mistaken.[2]

The Cuban question came to the front in the latter part of the Cleveland administration and there were excited demands for American recognition of Cuban independence. Rockhill became the target for considerable criticism because of his opposition. He felt certain that recognition of Cuban independence would result in war with Spain and should this occur, he thought there was some danger of European intervention. He did not like that part of the platform adopted by the Republicans at St. Louis which called for the employment of our good offices in Cuba "to restore peace and give independence to the island." Rockhill wrote: "They were put in it, I understand, by my friend Cabot Lodge. I do not think he distinguished himself by so doing!" [3]

Roosevelt had feared that Rockhill might be turned out if the Republicans should win the fall election. When the Republicans did win, Rockhill made an effort to get the appointment as Minister to China. General James Wilson, a friend since Legation days in Peking, campaigned for Rockhill. Other supporters included Senators Allison, Hale, and Lodge. A friend of Rockhill's wrote to Bellamy Storer, candidate for Rockhill's position as Assistant Secretary of State:

As you know he is one of the great authorities in the world on the subject of the East especially China and Japan and no one could be found so competent to represent our country in either of these situations. His intimate knowledge of languages, his experience in diplomacy and his long residence in those parts would enable him if sent to either of these empires to render inestimable services to our country. Spring once said to me that if Rockhill was in the English service he would be regarded as one of their greatest possessions.[4]

One of Rockhill's supporters wrote that President McKinley had stated that Rockhill would be appointed. Wilson, in May, 1897, reported that a group of prominent business men had spoken to the President in Rockhill's behalf. Wilson, the aggressive manager of the movement, wrote:

I congratulate you on the improved condition of your case, and as I am to meet Mr. Cook tomorrow afternoon at Cassatts with Thomas Griscom and all the . . . countryside, we will take counsel with each other as to the best means and the best men to put pressure on the part of our business interests upon the President.

If you can get your hands on Charles Cramp by all means press him into seeing the President in person. Meanwhile I will call upon Mr. Johnson and Mr. Search in the morning and organize a raid if I can in your behalf, without using any of our forces twice. . . .[5]

---

[2] Rockhill to C. W. Campbell, April 3, 1896, Rockhill Papers.

[3] Rockhill to General James H. Wilson, June 24, 1896, Rockhill Papers.

[4] Copy of a letter written to Bellamy Storer, February 11, 1897, Rockhill Papers.

[5] Wilson to Rockhill, May 12, 1897, Rockhill Papers.

Wilson also checked reports that certain of the missionary interests were opposed to Rockhill, considering this extremely important since the President was a Methodist.[6] But all efforts came to naught. On May 4 Edward Wolcott, wealthy corporation lawyer and Senator from Colorado, wrote to Henry White, Rockhill's colleague in the State Department, that Rockhill would not get the China post and that he was trying to have Rockhill appointed to Greece.[7] Mr. E. H. Conger, of Iowa, received the appointment coveted by Rockhill, reputedly because the President felt he had to appoint a western man.[8]

On May 10, 1897, Rockhill's services as Assistant Secretary of State came to an end. On July 8, McKinley appointed him Minister to Greece, Rumania, and Servia, a diplomatic post of no vital interest to the United States. Though Rockhill disliked the appointment, he had to accept for financial reasons.

In August, Rockhill and his wife met their two daughters at Naples—they had been attending school in France—and embarked on an Italian boat for Piraeus. It was an inauspicious beginning. The boat proceeded leisurely along the Sicilian coast, making frequent stops. More time was consumed in making a call at Crete. Hot weather and poor food robbed the trip of the pleasures associated with a Mediterranean cruise. Before reaching his destination, Rockhill was ill with ptomaine poisoning.

In Greece, in the autumn of 1897, intense heat added to the discomfiture of an uninspiring scene of poverty and of the military disaster suffered recently at the hands of the Turks. At his first audience with King George the condition of the palace, a "gaunt barrack-like building whose interior dilapidation was even worse than its forbidding and untended exterior," shocked Rockhill. During the conversation with the King, he was embarrassed to discover that he had a wad of horsehair in his hand; he had unconsciously plucked it from the worn chair in which he was sitting. Even more annoying was the sight of the returned soldiers—ragged and undisciplined, led by untidy, swaggering officers. In a dispatch to the Department of State, Rockhill reported:

> I beg to inform you as a matter of general interest that the disorganization of all branches of the government here resulting from the recent war is becoming more painfully evident every day. The Treasury is empty, and the various Departments unable in consequence to satisfactorily discharge the duties devolving upon them. The War and the Interior Departments are those most embarrassed. The former has been discharging the volunteers for the war and certain classes of the soldiers of the reserve, but is unable to give these men more than about $1.50 for their services, having deducted from the amount of pay due them, the value of their uniforms and outfit. As a result the streets are full of half uniformed men begging, and several riots have taken place in attempts to get bread and shelter.[9]

Thousands of refugees added to the scene of confusion in Athens.

---

[6] *Ibid.*, May 13, 1897.

[7] Edward Wolcott to Henry White, May 4, 1897, White Papers, Library of Congress.

[8] *Ibid.*, June 8, 1897.

[9] Rockhill to Secretary of State John Sherman, October 27, 1897, Department of State Archives.

The American Legation offered no oasis in this desert of decay. In his inventory of the furnishings, Rockhill recorded three office chairs, in poor condition, and one damaged desk. Even the simple necessities were lacking. To the Secretary of State, Rockhill wrote the following request for a typewriter: "Being also obliged to do all the copying in the record books—or in other words write over my compositions three times, it would be a great relief if I were able to do some of this mechanical work in a still more mechanical way." [10]

What little of interest Greece had to offer, Rockhill was in no mood to enjoy. While Mrs. Rockhill enthusiastically read everything she could find about the country, made sight-seeing trips, and attended lectures, her husband refused to go further than a day's journey from the Legation. He seemed to take some satisfaction in that, although he had been compelled to come to this awful country, at least he did not have to see it. When Henry Adams visited the family in the spring of 1898, he toured the country with Mrs. Rockhill and Dorothy. Rockhill remained at home except for a trip to Rumania and Servia with Adams. Rumania, and especially the Crown Princess (later Queen Marie), met with his approval, but he foresaw only trouble for the Balkans and was impressed by the danger to European peace.

Dust, heat, and day after day of glaring sunshine made Athens as uncomfortable as a desert during the summer of 1898. Early in the mornings or in the evenings, the Rockhills made short trips to the seashore; during the day they remained behind the closed windows and shutters of their house. They had made plans to go to Corfu, but Rockhill felt that he must remain at his post. On July 5, Mrs. Rockhill was taken ill with typhoid; she died two weeks later. Rockhill felt that in losing her he had lost everything. Dorothy later wrote:

> She was 43 years old, beautiful and gay, the most delightful companion and the most unselfish wife imaginable. During the 21 years she was married to my father she helped him in every way without a thought for herself. Where his intolerance antagonized, she would charm people back; she made friends for him; she gave him self-confidence when his modesty and shyness stood in his way; she smoothed the rough places (and there were a great many) and laughed at them with a sense of humor that, though sometimes biting, was never so where he was concerned. He had leaned on her in every way and when she died, I think he genuinely felt what he wrote to my grandmother Tyson: that she was the centre of his universe, and that in losing her he had lost everything.[11]

Athens was no longer bearable for Rockhill; he made every effort to escape. Shortly after Mrs. Rockhill's death, he and Dorothy spent two weeks in Constantinople, and in the autumn they went to Italy. On their return, Rockhill completed the task of translating and editing *The Journey of William of Rubruck to the Eastern Parts of the World,* written originally in Latin. In ad-

[10] *Ibid.,* November 16, 1898.

[11] Manuscript on the early life of her father, by Dorothy Rockhill.

dition he wrote extensive reports to the Department of State—confiding to Dorothy that probably no one would ever read them.

In the United States his friends, Henry Adams, John Hay, and probably Alvey A. Adee, a prominent career diplomat, did their best to have him appointed Librarian of Congress but Senator Lodge insisted on the appointment of a defeated Massachusetts politician. Rockhill considered a third trip of exploration and wrote to Theodore Roosevelt, who first tried to dissuade him but finally promised help. Then, on April 4, 1899, Rockhill received a telegram from Adee: "Your name suggested by friends director bureau american republics salary five thousand would you accept if appointed." Rockhill indicated his willingness, and, on April 10, received formal notice of appointment. On April 27 he left Athens for Washington. To his successor, Arthur S. Hardy, he wrote: "For my part, I cannot imagine anyone finding anything in such a stupid place to cause him to like it, unless all of their interests are archaeological." Rockhill was on the threshold of his career as a leading Far Eastern diplomat; his apprenticeship had come to an end.

Thirty years' study of the Orient hardly prepared Rockhill for a career in the Bureau of American Affairs. Although his friends undoubtedly looked upon the appointment as merely the most convenient way of getting him to Washington, he accepted with the hope that he might make the Bureau a vital force in improving inter-American relations. But demands on his time by the Department of State soon made it impossible for him to achieve this aim. Shortly after assuming his new duties, Rockhill received a note from his friend John Hay, who had become Secretary of State in the summer of 1898, asking him to look over some correspondence in regard to the Shanghai concession. Hay wrote that Adee "particularly desired before going away that the matter might be submitted to your judgement." [12]

During the next six years, Rockhill devoted most of his time to serving as a consultant on Far Eastern affairs and, in addition to the annual salary of $5,000 he received as Director of the Bureau of American Affairs, he was paid $3,000 a year by the Department of State.[13] Usually hard pressed financially, he was now free from financial worries, and he thoroughly enjoyed Washington. In most positions held hitherto he had complained of the stupid social life and the lack of work; he complained on neither score during his stay at the national capital.[14]

[12] Secretary of State John Hay to Rockhill, June 1, 1899, Rockhill Papers.

[13] Rockhill to Secretary of State Philander Knox, June 7, 1911, Rockhill Papers.

[14] His satisfaction with his work during this period is indicated in a letter to Hippisley. "The President some months ago told me he wanted me to go back to China as Minister as soon as he could get Conger out. I said I would go though I did not want the place at all but would much like to go to Japan. I know no more about it than that. For the time being—ever since my return home last autumn, I have held the confidential position of advisor to the Dept. of State on Chinese affairs. If I must meddle in Chinese matters I prefer to do so from Washington where I can more easily and effectively urge my views than

A new romance undoubtedly contributed to Rockhill's satisfaction with life in the United States. While he was still in Athens, Edith Perkins of Litchfield, Connecticut, and her father had called on Rockhill for assistance while they were touring the city. Rockhill was impressed by the beautiful and charming Edith, and before he left Athens he had dinner with her at least once. In the summer of 1899, he asked if he might visit her at Block Island. After that he went to Litchfield every other week-end. In his eagerness to please Edith and win her hand, he read his first and only novel—*Concerning Isabel Carnaby*—and became a staunch Episcopalian.

The wedding ceremony took place on April 25, 1900, in the Congregational church in Litchfield. The *New Haven Evening Register* reported that the ceremony "was attended by one of the largest and most fashionable assemblages which have graced an occasion of this kind in Connecticut for several years." The Congregational church—where during his first pastorate the great Lyman Beecher had preached hell-fire and brimstone—was hardly recognizable as a simple old meeting house. The *Litchfield Enquirer* recorded that, for the occasion, all the pulpit furniture had been removed from the platform, the two front pews taken away, and the low platform extended and surrounded with palms, Easter lilies, and white azaleas.

Following the ceremony, two hundred guests attended a reception at the Perkins' "fine colonial home." Telegrams of congratulation were read from the President, Cabinet members, members of the diplomatic corps, and many others "prominent not only in the official and social life of Washington and other cities in America, but also of several of the European, South American and Asiatic cities." In the afternoon the bride and groom left for an eleven-day trip through the Berkshires.

In the years ahead Edith won the admiration of her husband's colleagues by her graciousness and vivacious personality. Like the first Mrs. Rockhill, she never begrudged him the endless hours he gave to his studies nor, as far as outsiders could discern, did she become irritable when he wrapped himself in silence and in gloom for periods of days and even weeks.

---

from the Legation in Peking. There is a possibility of my going back to the Dept. as Assistant Sec. again for a while in case the present Assistant can be got out—he wants an Embassy—but as this will entail a serious loss of income for me, I don't care for it. However I shall go wherever I can be of most use to the Secretary and Roosevelt. . . ." Rockhill to Alfred E. Hippisley, August [?], 1902, Rockhill Papers.

CHAPTER FOUR

Writing the Open Door Policy

During the summer and fall of 1899, Rockhill scored his greatest diplomatic triumph—the writing of the Open Door notes. His arrival in Washington, early in the summer of 1899, coincided with a rapidly developing crisis in the Far East. Late in 1897 and early in 1898, Germany, Russia, France, and England forced China to grant them spheres of interest and influence. Authoritative opinion ventured that the Chinese Empire faced complete partition.

The extreme nationalism pervading the Western world in the late 1890's which found expression in the demands placed upon China had its counterpart in the United States where there was a growing public sentiment in favor of increased participation in world affairs. Rockhill's friends, Admiral Alfred Thayer Mahan, Theodore Roosevelt, and Henry Cabot Lodge, called for a stronger navy, naval bases, and a Nicaraguan canal. Lodge wrote: "The great nations are rapidly absorbing for their future expansion and their present defence all the waste places of the earth. It is a movement which makes for civilization and the advancement of the race. As one of the great nations of the world, the United States must not fall out of the line of march." [1] Lodge was not alone in seeing the situation as a final judgment on the nations of the world. Another writer in *The Forum* declared: "When we discuss the subject of National Expansion, we should do so in the light of one momentous fact, the greatest, the most profoundly significant, that has ever confronted the human race. It is this—that the movements now in progress are about to settle definitely, for the first time in history, the international relations of the whole earth." [2]

This atmosphere of crisis provided the backdrop for the war against Spain in 1898. The military mission to emancipate Cuba from Spanish atrocities culminated in the annexation of the Philippine Islands and Guam and hastened the acquisition of the Hawaiian Islands and the final settlement of the Samoan question.

Not since 1853, when Commodore Matthew C. Perry launched his program for an American empire in the Far East, had there been any serious move in that direction. Yet, in the brief span of the year 1898, the United States was convinced that the islands of the Far Pacific should be annexed. When a revolution in Hawaii in 1893 had catapulted the islands into American hands, the United States had just as abruptly declined to annex them, but in the summer

[1] Henry Cabot Lodge, "Our Blundering Foreign Policy," *The Forum,* March, 1895, p. 17.

[2] Samuel F. Moffett, "Ultimate World Politics," *The Forum,* August, 1899, p. 665.

of 1898 there was slight delay. The reversal was largely the result of two arguments presented to Congress: that these Pacific islands were necessary for protection against enemy attacks, and that they furnished the key to the potential markets of the Far East.

Concern for the China market for American goods accounted in considerable part for this sudden expansion of the American horizon. Lack of authoritative information on China's resources and the desire to see a potential market assured an easy passage of estimates and predictions from the realm of fact into the realm of fancy. Representative William Sulzer of New York, in advocating annexation of the Hawaiian Islands, indulged in roseate forecasting.

> Let me say to the business men of America, Look to the land of the setting sun, look to the Pacific! There are teeming millions there who will ere long want to be fed and clothed the same as we are. There is the great market that the continental powers are to-day struggling for. We must not be distanced in the race for the commerce of the world. In my judgment, during the next hundred years the great volume of trade and commerce, so far as this country is concerned, will not be eastward, but will be westward; will not be across the Atlantic, but will be across the broad Pacific. The Hawaiian Islands will be the key that will unlock to us the commerce of the Orient, and in a commercial sense make us rich and prosperous.[3]

Julius Pratt and A. Whitney Griswold have shown how the desire to protect the China market was a most important factor in the annexation of the Philippine Islands.[4]

Yet less than a year after the annexation of Hawaii and only a few months after the acquisition of the Philippines, it appeared that it would take more than these keys to keep the door to China open for Americans in the face of Europe's use of brute force. Newspapers expressed the concern. One editorial writer voiced great fear of Russian expansion in Manchuria where American trade had made the greatest advance. Why, he asked, would Russia want to acquire the Middle Kingdom if she was not to enjoy special trade privileges?[5] Another writer spoke of the trade opportunities in China and predicted that when the country was opened it would become one of the richest nations in the world. He concluded: "The 'open door' and the preservation of the integrity of China are of the highest importance to us, for we have a splendid opportunity to profit by the development of the country."[6] That the commercial motive

[3] *Congressional Record,* June 14, 1898 (Washington: Government Printing Office, 1898), p. 5906.

[4] Julius W. Pratt, *Expansionists of 1898* (Baltimore: The Johns Hopkins Press, 1936) and A. Whitney Griswold, *The Far Eastern Policy of the United States* (New York: Harcourt, Brace & Co., 1938).

[5] "A Russian Appeal for American Good Will," *New York Sun,* July 4, 1899, p. 6.

[6] "Into the Heart of China," *New York Sun,* June 4, 1899, p. 3.

On October 19, while the negotiations were in progress, Rockhill forwarded a resolution adopted by a convention of manufacturers and merchants meeting in Philadelphia. The convention, after reviewing the growing importance of the China market, resolved "that

played an important part in the China policy seems beyond dispute; however, this was only one factor.

Missionaries, like merchants, looked to the government for aid. By the end of the century, mission-minded Americans were contributing more than five million dollars annually for spreading the gospel, and they welcomed every step taken by the government to open China to foreigners. Merchants had given no more hearty approval to the system of extraterritoriality, for instance, than had the missionary and his supporters at home. With the granting of extraterritoriality, both the missionary and the native convert gained immunity from Chinese law, and, as one missionary wrote, it forced China "to see herself bound over by it unto the tutelage of her Conquerors."

The same missionary saw in the indignity imposed on China the force which would compel her to move toward Westernization, "by a revolution which shall touch every spring of her actions and have for its final outcome the uplifting of the nation to a higher plane of life and civilization." He likened extraterritoriality to an axe necessary for the clearing of the forest; and considered the treaty clause "so great and beneficent . . . that it might well be called the providential clause." It did much more than grant the missionary immunity from Chinese law. It had, he said:

> become a moral lever . . . in the hands of at least thirteen of the great nations of Christendom who were a unit in fixing it under China, and for thirty years have been a unit in maintaining it there. It is under the seat of government, and unless Christendom prove false to its unity, its pressure will not be removed till China has accepted our Christian civilization and is eligible to a place and recognition in the family and comity of Christian nations.[7]

Viewed in this light, Western imperialism was the force necessary to eradicate Chinese pride and superstition and thus open the door to Christianity. This was the religious version of Western colonialism, and clothed with piety and alleged beneficence it had a greater appeal than the cry for markets. The returning missionary, endowed with the prestige of having laid down his life to spread the gospel, reached the church-going public and built up an interest in China. The Department of State recognized this fact and trod warily where missionary interests were involved; but public interest in China enabled the government to undertake commitments there which would not have been tolerated if made in regard to Europe.

While it should not be exaggerated, the warm response with which the Open

---

an emphatic declaration should be made by the Government of the United States of its intention to protect to the fullest extent the rights which its citizens enjoy under existing treaties to pursue their trade in the Chinese Empire. . . ." In his letter, Rockhill wrote: "I am pleased to believe that they will be satisfied." W. W. Rockhill to Secretary of State John Hay, October 19, 1899, Hay Papers, Library of Congress. All Hay Papers cited hereafter are in the Library of Congress.

[7] *Records of the General Conference of the Protestant Missionaries of China held at Shanghai, May 7-20, 1890* (Shanghai: American Presbyterian Mission Press, 1890), p. 18.

Door notes were to be greeted is to be partly accounted for by the traditional antagonism toward Roman Catholics. The grabbing of spheres of influence in China in 1898 raised the question as to whether Protestant or Catholic countries would gain the lion's share. Writers in missionary periodicals posed this question. Action by the United States could be looked upon as a blow against popery, a consideration which appealed to sentiments more deeply rooted than any feeling against foreign entanglements.

The China question was of prime importance when Rockhill was appointed Far Eastern adviser to the Department of State. That American interests were at stake was clear; that time was running short was equally apparent. And the American temper of 1899 was not one of fateful resignation to a march of events destined to prove harmful.

Action was hastened by the arrival of Alfred E. Hippisley in Baltimore, his wife's home, in June, 1899. Hippisley, an Englishman who had served in the Chinese Maritime Customs since 1867 and had recently been stationed in Peking and Tientsin, wrote later that he was "so apprehensive regarding the future of China that my thoughts were chiefly occupied in trying to devise some scheme which would give China a breathing space in which she might put her house in order." [8] Fearing for China's future, Hippisley went to Washington to confer with his friend Rockhill. Rockhill was delighted; he had the greatest respect for Hippisley's opinions, and he was especially anxious to get a first-hand account of recent events in China.

Apparently this was the first time that they discussed the Open Door and the need for action. Rockhill and Hippisley had not met since the disastrous defeat of China in 1894-1895, and the correspondence of the two men had never touched upon the Open Door problem. Hippisley was not, in any sense, an emissary of the British government. That government had felt a deep concern for its historic policy of the Open Door and had approached the United States with a proposal for joint action. Hippisley preferred to have the United States take the initiative since the other powers were less suspicious of her than they were of England.[9] Rockhill had no desire to rake England's chestnuts out of the fire either, for he termed that country "as great an offender in China as Russia itself."

Rockhill and Hippisley approached the problem of formulating a policy for the United States with primary interest in staving off the threatened partition of China. Hippisley had no reason to be concerned with American interests in the Far East; and his absence from England since 1867 and deep love for China make it appear that he was moved only by a desire to save her.

What motivated Rockhill is less certain but there is sufficient evidence to permit reasonable speculation. He had no great interest in the promotion of American business and manifested even less sympathy with missionary enterprise.

[8] Alfred E. Hippisley to Norman Dwight Harris, May 31, 1921, Rockhill Papers.

[9] Hippisley to Rockhill, July 25, 1899, Rockhill Papers.

Of course, as an employee of the State Department he would of necessity have to subordinate these personal views.

The best clue to Rockhill's motives lies in an examination of his views on China. He was deeply distrustful of Chinese officials and he was too much a student to share in the contemporary sentimental feelings toward the Chinese people. He was not a reformer who "loved" the Chinese in the hope that he might reform them in the image of Westerners. But, while harboring a degree of disdain for individual Chinese, he nevertheless had great admiration for their civilization and strongly opposed the breakup of the Empire.

Viewing the scene in 1899, Rockhill saw the Western nations competing with each other in a race for spheres of influence. This rivalry enabled China to escape her obligations and resulted in failure to take any constructive steps in her own behalf. China had to be saved from partition; Rockhill believed that this could be done only if China became sufficiently strong to discharge her own responsibilities and to meet Western demands. She would not strengthen herself on her own initiative; she would not give an inch from her traditional ways unless compelled to do so. The rivalries among the Western powers must be halted and the combined pressure of the Western powers brought to bear on China, compelling her to take the steps necessary for her own protection.

As adviser to the Secretary of State, Rockhill had to put his case in terms of American interests. It was not difficult: should the race for spheres of influence continue and each nation exercise greater and greater control in its sphere, the China market soon would be closed to the American merchant.

Rockhill and Hippisley became co-workers on a design for the preservation of the Open Door and the integrity of the Chinese Empire. Not long after Hippisley met Rockhill in Washington, Rockhill introduced him to Secretary of State Hay. Hay, already convinced of the importance of the Open Door in China, was impressed with the views expressed by both experts but serious obstacles stood in the way of official action. Those responsible for foreign policy had to be as wary of what Hay termed "senseless prejudices" in the Senate and among the people as they had to be concerned about the vital interests of the nation.

In the letters exchanged by Rockhill and Hippisley during August, a policy gradually took form—the policy which was to become the guidepost for American diplomacy in the Orient during the twentieth century. When Rockhill returned to Washington on August 3, after a brief vacation in Litchfield, he found a letter from Hippisley. It was Hippisley's opinion that spheres of interest must be recognized as existing facts and that the exclusive railroad and mining privileges of the controlling powers must also be accepted. However, no one of the powers had yet claimed the right to have its goods enter its own sphere in China subject to lower duties than goods of other nations, although this privilege would also soon be claimed. It remained for the United States then to secure from each of the powers an assurance that the "Chinese treaty tariff shall without discrimination apply to all merchandise entering the spheres of influence;

and that any treaty ports in them shall not be interfered with." [10] Hippisley thought that this was all that could be done at this late date but that such a guarantee of equality of opportunity for all commerce would be a major achievement.

Rockhill wished to go further and proposed that the United States also express its interest in China's independence and integrity. He wrote: "You know what my views are about the position the United States should take in China: I would like to see it make a declaration in some form or other, which would be understood by China as a pledge on our part to assist in maintaining the integrity of the empire." [11] Thus it was Rockhill—not Hippisley—who linked the Open Door policy with the territorial integrity of China. To offer a pledge for China's integrity was a corollary of no small importance.

A second letter from Hippisley, written on August 16, urged action. Rockhill had expressed fear that any move would be interpreted as following the British line, and that the politicians would hesitate to lay themselves open to this charge before the next year's election. Hippisley cleverly replied that events in China would soon force the administration to take some action to protect the interests of the American exporters. In the meantime England might act and leave the administration open to the charge it so much wished to avoid.[12]

Rockhill was so impressed with both of Hippisley's letters that he decided to forward long extracts to Alvey Adee of the State Department, but, in replying to Hippisley, he returned to the subject of the corollary he had earlier proposed.

> I can not, however, think that, at the present stage, it will be sufficient for this country to insist that no discrimination shall apply to any of our merchandise entering the various spheres of interest. We must go much farther than that. Our action, to my mind, should be such that the very vague assurances given by Great Britain, Russia, and other powers as to their desire to maintain and insure the integrity of the Chinese Empire, should be expressed in much stronger terms and assume tangible shape.[13]

Hippisley replied that he had been hesitant to broach the subject in view of the administration's lukewarm attitude toward taking any action whatsoever, but now that the United States no longer had any reason to fear Russian opposition in view of the Czar's ukase of August 15 declaring Talienwan a free port, perhaps McKinley and Hay would be less reluctant to act. Moreover, the article in the *North American Review* by Prince Ookhtomsky, a man supposedly close to the Czar, seemed to assure respectful Russian consideration for a proposal to insure China's independence and integrity.[14] Hippisley, accordingly, included in his memorandum for Rockhill the provision that China should collect the duties within the spheres of influence.[15]

[10] *Ibid.*

[11] Rockhill to Hippisley, August 3, 1899, Rockhill Papers.

[12] Hippisley to Rockhill, August 16, 1899, Rockhill Papers.

[13] Rockhill to Hippisley, August 18, 1899, Rockhill Papers.

[14] Vladmir Holmstrem, "*Ex Oriente Lux!* A Plea for a Russo-American Understanding," with an Introduction by Prince E. Ookhtomsky, *North American Review*, July, 1899, p. 7.

[15] Hippisley to Rockhill, August 21, 1899, Rockhill Papers.

When Rockhill and his friend first exchanged views they had little hope that the State Department would follow their suggestions. Early in August, Rockhill started working on a magazine article with the purpose of arousing public opinion. By August 28, however, happenings beyond the ken of Rockhill and Hippisley had dissipated the fears of the administration, and no longer did the "senseless prejudices" stand in the way. The willingness of the McKinley administration to act appears to have been hastened by indications that Russia would grant respectful consideration to a proposal, and by the opinions of Dr. Jacob Gould Schurman, President of Cornell University, who, on his return from the Philippines, voiced great concern for the future of American trade in China.

Rockhill's memorandum to Hay did not differ essentially from the one he had received from Hippisley; this is not surprising in view of the fact that the Englishman had incorporated all of Rockhill's suggestions. In addition, it reviewed the arguments of Lord Charles Beresford in his book, *The Break-Up of China.* Rockhill disagreed with Beresford only by denying the necessity of making China a military and naval power.[16] Rockhill placed special emphasis on the necessity of recognizing as fact the existing spheres of interest.

Rockhill's memorandum received the approval of the administration, and he was commissioned to draft the dispatches to be forwarded to Great Britain, Russia, Germany, and France. Except for slight changes in word order and in form, the dispatches sent were identical with Rockhill's drafts. These notes asked each of the powers to declare that it would not interfere with any vested interest within its own sphere of interest or leased territory. Similarly the nations were asked to commit themselves not to discriminate against citizens of other nations in the matter of harbor dues or railway rates.

The remaining point in the Open Door notes calls for special emphasis. It specified that the Chinese treaty tariff should apply within each sphere of interest and that the Chinese government should collect the duties. While this would help preserve equal commercial opportunities, it would also—and from Rockhill's point of view this was all important—preserve China's jurisdiction in the territories in question. Rockhill wrote: "It furthermore has the advantage of insuring to the United States the appreciation of the Chinese Government, who would see in it a strong desire to arrest the disintegration of the Empire and would greatly add to our prestige and influence at Peking." [17]

Although the Open Door notes of 1899 had as their aim the preservation of Chinese sovereignty in the spheres of influence as well as equal commercial opportunity, this objective was merely implied. Rockhill would have preferred an open and unqualified statement on China's territorial and administrative integrity. To Hippisley he wrote: "The other side of the Chinese question is so awfully big, that I think for the time being we had better not broach it out here. All we can do, it seems to me, is to instruct our Legation out there to adopt a

[16] Rockhill memorandum to Hay, August 28, 1899, Rockhill Papers.

[17] *Ibid.*

general line of policy which may be favorable to the maintenance and the strengthening of the Peking Government." [18]

Hippisley was anxious to learn President McKinley's reaction to the "independence & integrity" portion. It was, he thought, the only one that might cause difficulty—and that only because the Chinese were so foolish. In concluding his letter, he sounded a note of optimism. "But if the gov'ts. can agree among themselves to respect the integrity & independence of China, it should not be difficult for them to bring sufficient pressure to bear on China to induce her to embark on a real course of progress." [19] It has often been overlooked that the notes went beyond a bare attempt to guarantee freedom of trade. Rockhill had already taken a big step toward the forthright position announced by Secretary Hay in July, 1900.[20]

Rockhill played the key role in the negotiations which followed the sending of dispatches. In October he received a reply from Lord Salisbury asking if the term "leased territory" could be omitted from the declaration, hoping thereby to exclude both Kowloon and Weihaiwei. Rockhill advised Adee that the British request was reasonable in that foreigners would be accorded the same rights in Kowloon as in Hongkong while there was no trade in Weihaiwei.[21] But as Tsingtao and Kiaochow were also leased territories, to accede to the British request would be to emasculate the policy. Accordingly, the reply to Lord Salisbury requested that leased territories be included.[22]

While the Czar's ukase inspired the hope that Russia would readily ascribe to the principles laid down in the Open Door notes, Rockhill found Cassini, the Russian Ambassador in Washington, difficult to convince. In his first conversation with Rockhill, Cassini stated that Russia could not bind herself in giving any pledges concerning leased territory. Kwantung was, for the term of the

[18] Rockhill to Hippisley, September 14, 1899, Rockhill Papers.

[19] Hippisley to Rockhill, September 14, 1899, Rockhill Papers.

[20] Writers have overlooked this aspect and have uniformly stated that the sole aim was to preserve equality of commercial opportunity. Griswold, in his excellent study, *The Far Eastern Policy of the United States,* writes: "The notes, like the memoranda from which they were written, and as their authors had privately agreed, eschewed the subject of China's territorial integrity." They avoided a forthright statement on this point but this does not mean that they avoided the subject. The Rockhill papers *establish as a fact* that the notes aimed to preserve China's integrity and independence.

That the author of the Open Door notes thought in terms of something more than protection of American commerce is apparent in a letter he wrote to Secretary Hay during the Boxer negotiations. He observed: "Altogether Russia is having and will in all probability continue to have everything her own way in this part of the world. Fortunately she will not be for many years to come a serious competitor for the trade of Eastern Asia and so, if our interests out here are purely commercial—which I do not however think they are, we may still confidently expect our China trade to go on increasing." Rockhill to Hay, January 29, 1901, Hay Papers.

[21] Rockhill memorandum to Alvey A. Adee, Rockhill Papers.

[22] Rockhill draft of instructions to Joseph Choate, Rockhill Papers.

lease, an integral part of the Russian Empire and under Russian law. In his report to the Secretary of State, Rockhill expressed the opinion that Russia probably would demand preferential rights in her leased territory.[23]

In a second conversation with Rockhill, the Russian Ambassador raised the question of Great Britain's possible role in the sending of the Hay notes, now commonly called the Open Door notes. Was not Great Britain coquetting with the United States? Had the notes been sent at her suggestion? Rockhill ridiculed the idea; no administration in the United States could afford to leave itself open to such a charge. Cassini then questioned Great Britain's sincerity in her espousal of the Open Door. Rockhill parried this charge with the statement that if Great Britain was not favorable this was an opportune moment to bring pressure on her, and should Russia be the first to accept the Hay proposal it "would have as favorable an effect on the final acceptance of the policy by all powers as it would if England were the first to declare it."[24]

By the middle of December, all of the powers with the exception of Russia had accepted. Rockhill once again went to see Cassini and made full use of the fact that only Russia had failed to agree. The President, he said, might report to Congress in the near future—and it would be embarrassing to report that Russia alone had not replied. This would create suspicion of Russia among the American people. Rockhill also argued that unity among the treaty powers would bring an end to the Chinese policy of playing one against the other.[25]

The replies to the Hay notes were evasive. Great Britain agreed to the proposals only after the United States met her insistence that Kowloon be excluded by suggesting that no mention be made of this leasehold.[26] Germany also agreed, but, anxious to avert a controversy among the European nations, advised that she did not think it would be wise to press the powers for specific commitments.[27] A note was not dispatched to France until November 21. A month later she accepted the general proposal but carefully omitted any reference to "spheres of influence." [28] Italy and Japan also received the Hay notes in November, and both countries accepted without qualification.

Russia, faced with the acceptance of the Hay proposals by the other powers, finally accepted, but, to Hay and Rockhill, her reply was the least satisfactory. From her declaration she specifically excluded leased territories, stating that it was for China to settle the question of custom duties in open ports and that

[23] Rockhill memorandum to Hay, December 12, 1899, Rockhill Papers.

[24] *Ibid.*

[25] *Ibid.*, December 19, 1899.

[26] Joseph Choate to Hay, November 1, 1899, Hay Papers; quoted by Alfred L. P. Dennis, *Adventures in American Diplomacy, 1896-1906* (New York: E. P. Dutton & Co., 1928), p. 189.

[27] Andrew D. White to Hay, January 25, 1900, Rockhill Papers.

[28] Horace Porter to Hay, December 18, 1899, Department of State Archives; quoted by Dennis, *op. cit.*, p. 192.

Russia would claim no special privileges for her own subjects.[29] Hay hoped to give this Russian declaration the broadest possible interpretation. Since Count Muraviev, Russian Foreign Minister, during conversations with United States Ambassador Charlemagne Tower, had stated that Russia would do whatever France did, Hay planned to interpret the declaration in a broader way than the text itself would warrant.[30]

Qualified as the various replies were, neither Hay nor Rockhill thought it wise to press the matter further. Rockhill wrote to Hippisley that

> the powers have practically accepted the proposals of the United States, although I am fain to admit that the acceptance of Russia is not as complete as I would like it; in fact, it has what we call in America a string attached to it. Nevertheless, I think it prudent to accept it, for none of the European Powers are prepared to have this question made a subject of heated debate and controversy, and those who have given their unconditional acceptance of Mr. Hay's proposals would withdraw them if they perceived that the Powers might get arrayed in hostile camps against each other on this subject.[31]

Late in January Ambassador Andrew D. White reported that Count von Bülow had said Germany did not wish to become involved in any controversy where she would have to take sides "as, for example, if England were on one side and France and Russia on the other, she would not wish to be drawn into a position where she must take sides." [32] No nation wished to jeopardize its position in Europe by taking a strong stand for full compliance with the request of Hay. Rockhill accepted the situation without complaint, apparently convinced that the main objective had been achieved.

Mindful of the fact that Japan was unprepared to compete in a race to divide China into colonial areas, Viscount Aoki, Japan's Foreign Minister, inquired regarding the answers sent to the United States. The head of Japan's Foreign Office saw in the answers "no more than declarations of the intention of these Powers to apply the most favored nation treatment to all nations. . . . " They did not, Aoki said, contain categorical replies to the three propositions contained in the original American proposals. Rockhill instructed the American Ambassador to Japan, Alfred E. Buck, to state that his government "did not seek to obtain replies from the various Powers . . . couched in identical terms, all that it desired was written declarations of intention. . . ." [33] This, said Rockhill, was the main object of the proposals.

Until the recent war brought about a greatly altered situation demanding a fresh assessment of American interests in the Pacific and a new appraisal of the

---

[29] Charlemagne Tower to Hay, January 2, 1900, Hay Papers; quoted by Tyler Dennett, *John Hay: From Poetry to Politics* (New York: Dodd, Mead & Co., 1933), p. 293.

[30] Hay to Tower, January 22, 1900, Hay Papers; quoted by Dennett, *op. cit.,* pp. 293-94.

[31] Rockhill to Hippisley, January 16, 1900, Rockhill Papers.

[32] White to Hay, January 25, 1900, Rockhill Papers.

[33] "Draft of reply to Mr. Buck's No. 434 of June 1, 1900," Rockhill Papers.

powerful forces operating in Asia, the Rockhill policy served as the basic plan for American diplomacy in the Far East. Rockhill would have been the first to call for a revision of policy to fit the new facts; he never considered his policy a permanent guiding principle. In his letter to John Hay submitting the Open Door memorandum, Rockhill spoke of "what I conceive to be the main points of the negotiations for a kind of *modus vivendi* in China." It was clear to Rockhill that China had not been finally rescued, and that an important American market had not been preserved for the indefinite future by one diplomatic maneuver. He believed, however, that by the proposals and their acceptance, the United States now held the balance of power.

> I hope sincerely that we may make good use of it, not only for our trade, but for strengthening the Peking Government so that it can find no means of escaping the performance of all its obligations to the Treaty Powers. What we have obtained will undoubtedly help to insure, for the time being, the integrity of the Chinese Empire, but, on its side, China can and must discharge its international obligations.[34]

In the diplomatic struggles of the next few years the United States made a fight for the fulfillment of the promise embodied in the policy of Rockhill and Hippisley—and no one played a more prominent part in that fight than Rockhill.

---

[34] Rockhill to Edwin Denby, January 13, 1900, Rockhill Papers.

CHAPTER FIVE

Rockhill's Influence on the Boxer Negotiations

The negotiations that followed the sending of the Open Door notes were not yet completed when the Chinese threatened to drive Westerners from the country. In a land where "procreative recklessness," as J. O. P. Bland termed it, always outran the capacity to produce the necessities of life, and where famines were frequent, disturbances characterized by looting and varying degrees of terrorism were inevitable. Crop failures in 1899 followed closely upon the buccaneering activities of Western statesmen in 1898. When mounting taxes resulting from the action of the foreign powers added to the burden, resentment against foreigners mounted to hatred. The logical Chinese reasoned that the best solution to the problem was to drive "the foreign devil" into the sea.

The Boxer movement started in Shantung in the fall of 1899 and, in the spring of the following year, spread throughout northern China, finally culminating in the siege of the legations in Peking. For two months in the summer of 1900, the world received only one message from the foreign legations at Peking. A telegraphic report from the American Minister, E. H. Conger, told the grim story of the siege by Boxers and national troops.[1] This grave message said that the Americans had retreated to the British Legation and only quick relief could prevent general massacre. On all sides Chinese forces pressed in, employing artillery and the full implements of war. In fear of them, 400 foreigners, including 200 women and children, retreated to the confines of the British Legation, which had been made into a veritable fortress. The besieged diplomats, missionaries, and newspaper correspondents built barricades with carts and furniture. They used all manner of textile furnishings to make sandbags. They built bombproof cellars and dug tunnels to prevent the Chinese from mining the crowded quarters. By the ninth of August, 60 had been killed and 120 wounded, and food for the stricken had been reduced to half portions of horse flesh.[2] In addition to the 400 besieged in the British Legation there were 1,000 foreigners and 3,000 Chinese converts in the remainder of the foreign legation area of Peking. Another 3,000 native Christians were besieged in the Pehtang cathedral. The attack on the cathedral was especially furious; 43 French and Italian sailors and more than 400 Chinese lost their lives. The outside world was horrified.

[1] U.S. Department of State, *Papers Relating to the Foreign Relations of the United States: 1900,* p. 156. These annual reports are hereafter cited as *Foreign Relations.*

[2] *Ibid.,* p. 159.

The Boxer movement caught the diplomats in China and the world-at-large unprepared. Antiforeign outbreaks had so many times threatened Westerners in China, only to sputter and then die out without serious consequences, that the foreign offices of the West viewed the first rumblings of the revolt in Shantung with equanimity. As late as June 1, Rockhill advised Hay: "I cannot believe that the 'Boxer' movement will be very long-lived or cause any serious complications. The day the Chinese authorities choose to put an end to it they can easily do so. I think they have now realized that they must act, and they will." [3] Rockhill, like so many Western experts on China, misjudged the situation. The Manchus and the Chinese authorities gave no evidence of being about to act in the spring of 1900; nor was there much reason to believe, on the basis of their attitude toward the revolt during the preceding months, that they would do so.

Partial helplessness, political expediency, and resentment at the cavalier way in which China had been treated were among the reasons why the authorities at Peking refrained from taking strong measures against the Boxers. That China could ill afford to permit a fanatical crusade against foreigners seems to have made no impression on the hard-pressed and increasingly impotent Manchu dynasty, which, from the first uprising of the Boxers in October, 1899, pursued a dilatory course. Although troops were sent against the Boxers, this official rebuke was seriously compromised by the government's support of the pro-Boxer Governor of Shantung province.[4] In drafting a protest against China's failure to protect the treaty rights of Americans who were being victimized, Rockhill called attention to the support the Governor was giving the Boxers. The pre-emptory reply of the central government was ill advised. On presenting the protest, Conger was told that he should advise the missionaries to restrain their converts and keep them in order and not permit them again to cause trouble.[5] As a result of foreign protests, the Governor of Shantung was finally removed from office, but the effect of this measure was nullified by his appointment to the Governorship of Shansi, a province where there were large foreign interests.[6] The early months of 1900 found the Peking government still avoiding the responsibilities imposed upon it in the foreign treaties.

Rockhill knew that an antiforeign movement of serious proportions would wipe out the gains made the previous year. Conger was advised to avail himself of every opportunity to impress upon the Tsungli Yamen, China's Foreign Office, the full significance of the recent action by the United States. In an instruction to Conger, Rockhill referred to the assurances which had been obtained from the various powers concerning freedom of trade in the leased territories and spheres of influence and the maintenance therein of China's rights of sovereignty. Rock-

[3] W. W. Rockhill to Secretary of State John Hay, June 1, 1900, Hay Papers.

[4] *Foreign Relations: 1900*, p. 77.

[5] *Ibid.*, pp. 81-82.

[6] *Ibid.*, p. 112.

hill stated that the declarations constituted a fresh promise on the part of the powers that they would in no way interfere with the integrity of China. He advised that, should the Chinese fail to protect the rights of foreigners, disaster might overtake the country.

Should the Chinese Government disregard these treaty duties, it is greatly to be feared that the policy now so happily inaugurated through the instrumentality of this Government will not bear the fruit which, under other circumstances, it might, and that further guarantees in the nature of occupation points within the limits of the Chinese Empire will speedily be demanded by European Powers, the disintegration of China hastened, if not precipitated, the Empire disturbed and rebellion brought about.[7]

These words of advice went unheeded in the Manchu-Chinese capital, and events rushed on to catastrophe.

The siege of the legations in Peking in the summer of 1900 raised problems of the first magnitude. The lives of the diplomatic representatives and the thousands of foreign and native refugees were in danger. Their rescue furnished the immediate problem. Scarcely less pressing was the danger that the powers would find in the Peking tragedy a pretext for the final breakup of the Empire. The foreign offices, excited by the supposed wealth of China, were in an aggressive mood. There was probably no nation which would choose to abstain, once the carving of the Chinese melon was under way. All that Rockhill had labored to achieve in the Open Door notes of 1899 was at stake.

The policy which Rockhill had drafted and Hay had sponsored during the twelve months prior to the outbreak served the purposes of the United States better than its author could have foreseen. The notes of 1899 had made clear to the world the position of the United States, and the halfhearted replies of the other powers had committed them to the principle of the Open Door, no matter how vague and halfhearted those commitments were. The United States undoubtedly would oppose any move threatening her own commercial interests in China. It had been implied that the United States considered the maintenance of China's territorial and administrative integrity necessary for the preservation of those commercial interests. On July 3, Hay went a step further, and, in a circular note to the powers, openly stated what previously had been left to conjecture: the United States sought a solution which might preserve China's territorial and administrative entity.[8]

During the anxious days of June and July, 1900, while the world awaited news from Peking, Hay treated the revolt as an insurrection by a minority of the people and declared that the purpose of the United States was to deal with China as a friendly nation.[9] At a time when few believed that the lives of the diplomats

[7] Rockhill to Hay, March 21, 1900, "Draft of Instructions to U.S. Minister at Peking," Rockhill Papers.

[8] *Foreign Relations: 1900,* p. 299.

[9] *Ibid.*

had been spared, Hay asserted that they were still alive, basing his belief on a message from Conger. The authenticity of this message was seriously open to question.[10] The outbreak could hardly be called an insurrection, since Chinese forces, backed by the Imperial government, were attacking the legations as if they were enemy bastions. Under normal circumstances such action would have been considered an act of war. Hay rejected this consideration only because war with China did not suit the purposes of American diplomacy. War was avoided, as Hay had hoped, but the decisive factor was the rivalry of the European nations, and not the action of the American Secretary of State.[11]

A force of two thousand marines and sailors from the Japanese and Western warships at Taku advanced toward Peking on June 9. Meeting unexpectedly strong Chinese opposition, the expedition had to retreat to Tientsin. Realizing that the situation was much more critical than they had hitherto suspected, the powers now began to organize a stronger force.

Political considerations, however, remained paramount during preparations for the new expedition. The chief difficulty was disagreement on the size of the contingents of each nation. Japan was in a position to send all the necessary forces at once. Since independent action would furnish the other powers with a precedent for taking advantage of the revolt to realize their imperialistic aims, she was unwilling to move without the concurrence of the other interested nations.[12] Therefore, on July 6, the Tokyo Foreign Office sought the consent of Great Britain, the United States, France, Russia, and Germany. Great Britain, not unmindful that the presence of Japanese troops would serve as a check on Russia, was anxious to have Japan go ahead.[13] The United States gave its approval, subject to the assent of the other powers.[14] Germany and Russia rejected the Japanese proposition, thereby postponing the rescue of the legations possibly for two weeks or even longer. Not until August 6, when the contingents of the Western nations were at last available, did the relief expedition depart from Tientsin.[15] Eight days later, on August 14, the legations were rescued.

It was at this juncture that President McKinley and Secretary Hay decided that Rockhill should go to China as Commissioner for the United States. Theodore Roosevelt, recently nominated for the Vice-Presidency, gave his hearty approval.

---

[10] Tyler Dennett, *John Hay: From Poetry to Politics* (New York: Dodd, Mead & Co., 1933), pp. 304-05.

[11] Although there are no documents indicating that Hay was acting on the advice of Rockhill in June, 1900, this seems possible in view of his depending heavily on Rockhill both before and after this time.

[12] *Foreign Relations: 1900,* p. 361.

[13] Great Britain, Parliamentary Papers, China No. 3 (1900); cited by Seiji G. Hishida, *The International Position of Japan as a Great Power* (New York: Columbia University Press, 1905), p. 211.

[14] *Foreign Relations: 1900,* p. 367.

[15] Hishida, *op. cit.,* pp. 211-12.

I felt as if a load were off my mind when it was announced that you were to go to China. "All things come to him who waits and works while waiting." Of course you should have been sent to China three years ago but it is all right to have you there now. I have not any but the most muddled idea as to what is to happen to China and as I will have to take the stump I shall be very grateful for any hints you can give me.[16]

Rockhill's appointments almost invariably led to protests from the missionaries. Hay quieted President McKinley's fears of political repercussions. During a close intimacy of several years, and "during almost constant conversations of the last year on Chinese matters," Hay told the President, he had never heard a word from Rockhill which offered any basis for believing that he would fail to defend the interests of the missionary. "I imagine the feeling towards him on the part of some of the Missionary Boards—not all of them by any means—arises from the fact that he has been a profound student of oriental theologies and has studied them from the point of view of history and philosophy, instead of sectarianism." [17]

Rockhill arrived at Shanghai on August 29, and proceeded immediately to Peking. His survey of conditions in that war-torn city led him to urge that American troops remain there.[18] Concerning Minister Conger he was lavish in his praise, describing him as "in all probability the ablest foreign representative in Peking, dispassioned, careful and clear sighted." With an enthusiasm most unusual for him, Rockhill wrote to Hay: "We have hit it off admirably; nothing could have exceeded the cordiality of his reception and the gracefulness of his accepting me as a cooperator. It might have been so awkward for both of us!" [19]

At the close of September, Rockhill returned to Shanghai for a brief visit before sailing up the Yangtze to visit the viceroys at Nanking and Hankow. He dined with Sir Ernest Satow, who was on his way to represent Great Britain at Peking. Rockhill later informed Hay that the Britisher "felt so convinced that the policy of his government was identical with that of the U.S., that he begged me to tell the Viceroys Liu Kim-yi and Chang Chih-tung when I saw them that he wished them to accept what I might have to tell them as embodying also the views of the British Government." [20]

Autumn was already in the air when Rockhill and his bride, Edith, boarded an American naval vessel bound for Nanking. The Boxer revolt had not spread to the Yangtze Valley and Rockhill hoped to ward off any danger of uprisings by conferring with the able viceroys there. He also desired their point of view before negotiations began at Peking.

No mission better suited Rockhill's talents. Understanding the Chinese love

[16] Theodore Roosevelt to Rockhill, July 21, 1900, Rockhill Papers.

[17] Hay to President William McKinley, July 23, 1900, Hay Papers.

[18] *Foreign Relations: 1900,* pp. 205-06.

[19] Rockhill to Hay, October 3, 1900, Hay Papers.

[20] *Ibid.*

of ceremony, he mustered all the pomp at his disposal. He pressed several Westerners into serving as his personal staff. At Hankow, the U.S.S. *Nashville* tendered the Viceroy, Chang Chih-tung, so enthusiastic a salute that it almost blew his gaily robed entourage into the water. At each city Rockhill and the viceroys exchanged calls, and Rockhill engaged each of them in confidential talks in Chinese.[21] On returning to Shanghai, Mrs. Rockhill wrote: "Will also feels well satisfied with his trip, and feels that these men *may* be able to save the situation, at all events, he has gotten in touch with the Chinese side of the question."

In Peking, Conger was dismayed by the task facing him in the negotiations. During Rockhill's absence, he wrote to Hay:

> As yet none of the powers has appointed other than their ministers to negotiate, or sent advisers or counsel, and I should not like to be the only one for whom such support is deemed necessary. But, realizing the unusual difficult problem before me, and knowing Mr. Rockhill's familiarity with the views and policies of the Department of State and his experiences in important diplomatic work, I should like very much to have his assistance, and hope he has already been instructed to join me.[22]

Late in October, Rockhill received orders to return to Peking, where negotiations were proceeding at tortoise pace.

The Rockhills went from Shanghai to Taku on a freight steamer loaded with wood and coal oil. With an immense iron lighter in tow, the ship made slow progress. There were no facilities for passengers, and the Rockhills had to provide their own mattresses, dishes, knives and forks, blankets, coffee, tea, and potted cream. To add to the discomfiture of Mrs. Rockhill, the crew smoked cigarettes night and day, and mindful of the inflammable cargo, she confessed that "it made her hair stand on end." Tientsin was still occupied by foreign troops when the Rockhills arrived there after a train trip from Taku. Mrs. Rockhill described the city as a "state of robbery, confusion, disorder, and disgrace." Peking seemed more tranquil. There they settled in the three rooms Rockhill had built for himself while he was Second Secretary of Legation.

The Peking Conference presented all the elements of an *opéra bouffe* with little men playing with the future destiny of four hundred million Chinese as if the Chinese did not matter. For a full year the diplomats bickered and delayed, and finally arranged a settlement characterized by lack of foresight, understanding, and common standards of honesty. Rockhill complained bitterly of the blundering ways in which the conference dealt with the Chinese. An entire month was wasted in drawing up indictments against men whose guilt had long since been proclaimed by the Chinese. Diplomats were not alone in their demand

[21] The facts of Rockhill's trip up the Yangtze are from a copy of a letter written by Mrs. Rockhill from Nanking to her family in Litchfield, Connecticut. The copy fails to give the date of writing. Copies of the letters written by Mrs. Rockhill from China were lent to the author by Miss Marion Crutch of Litchfield.

[22] *Foreign Relations: 1901,* Appendix, p. 43.

for punishment. Rockhill wrote to Hay: "Nearly daily some of our missionaries presents to Conger lists of persons they wish put to death, the evidence of these officials guilt being furnished them by native Christians. It is extraordinary to see such grave responsibility assumed with such lightheartedness. The missionaries—Catholic and Protestant, are the most bloodthirsty, vindictive lot at present." [23]

The American representative, Conger, had an abundance of good will toward the Chinese, but, not speaking French, the language used in the meetings, he was compelled to sit through the sessions without the slightest notion as to what was being said. At times the Belgian Minister translated for Conger's benefit. On one occasion Conger sought permission to have Rockhill at his side as interpreter, but this request was denied since no nation was deemed to be entitled to two representatives. The unfortunate Conger on occasion voted without knowing what he was voting for and, in the end, was so frustrated that he begged to be relieved.

The cavalier treatment accorded Conger left Rockhill in the position of advising a man unable to tell him what was under discussion. Only by consulting with the various representatives outside of the meetings was Rockhill able to keep himself informed.

The conference impressed Rockhill as "a miserable muddle." The various ministers were inept, lacking in determination, and did not even enjoy the confidence of their own governments. They were adamant in demanding punishment of the Chinese leaders—even going so far as to decree the death penalty for those who had been killed during the hostilities—but they failed to seize the golden opportunity to press for long-needed reforms in the Chinese government. To Rockhill it seemed that this was the proper time to encourage China to develop her own resources. He was especially interested in improving mining laws so that the government might enlarge its revenues. This also seemed the appropriate occasion to force the Chinese to set aside the Empress Dowager and to bring to an end the subsidies to the Manchus, a terrific drain on the treasury which Rockhill was convinced "should be put to better use than to maintain in idleness a couple of millions of drones." [24]

Rockhill and Conger were under instructions to fight for the Open Door and the strengthening of China. When Conger was subjected to criticism in the American press, Rockhill came to his defense, writing to Hay that Conger had done his best to carry out instructions, frequently "under considerable difficulty, for we must realize that the policy of the United States . . . is not very acceptable to any of the Powers none of whom care overmuch for the integrity of China or the maintenance of the *status quo* or the open door though they may openly advocate it at present." [25]

---

[23] Rockhill to Hay, February 4, 1901, Hay Papers.

[24] *Ibid.*

[25] *Ibid.*, February 18, 1901.

These were much too ethereal aims for the powers. Large indemnities and territory seemed infinitely more valuable than a strong China. Nor was all of the attention centered on China. Wherever three or more Europeans were gathered together, there was the inevitable consideration given to alignments in Europe. Rockhill observed that "The French Minister is apparently willing to do anything which puts the German in a false position, and the British is delighted to do the same as regards Russia." [26] Most dangerous was Russia. She occupied all of Manchuria and sought to arrange for a cession of that territory. When that plan fell through, it seemed to Rockhill that the Russian representative was "perfectly willing to see negotiations . . . drag on indefinitely, and to help waste as much time as possible over details of no special importance." [27] His observations concerning Germany also portended evil: "The German Minister is apparently hampered at every turn by his military men. The policy of Germany out here seems to be to secure control of the Diplomatic negotiations through the preponderance of its military." [28] Even Japan, hitherto cooperative, appeared to be ready to go along with the European nations if they would allot her the territory she wanted in China.[29] Only the ineptitude of the diplomats and mutual jealousy of the powers stood in the way of a grand barbecue where the Chinese dragon would be torn limb from limb. Rockhill was disgusted.

Finally, in February, Conger decided to bear the odium of leaving before the work was done rather than fail to defend the interests of the United States, and he asked for a short leave.[30] It was granted, and, on February 24, Rockhill assumed the responsibility for the American side of the negotiations. Almost at once he became a member of four committees and a leader in the Conference of Ministers. Mrs. Rockhill was exuberant over her husband's new role, and wrote: "Will has been at several more meetings, and enjoys the work very much and is head over heels in it. I hardly see him anymore these days." A few weeks later she told of his interest in the work and their mutual happiness and contentment.

Because of his friendship with Hay, Rockhill enjoyed unusual freedom in carrying on negotiations. His instructions from the Secretary were in general terms only; on occasion he made important decisions without referring to Washington; and late in the negotiations he even rejected several suggestions made by Hay. Briefly stated, his instructions were to pay special attention to the Open Door, seek to provide for the future security of merchants and missionaries, support the establishment of a minister of foreign affairs for China, de-

[26] *Ibid.*, April 18, 1901.

[27] *Ibid.*

[28] *Ibid.*

[29] *Ibid.*, January 9, 1901.

[30] Rockhill to Alfred E. Hippisley, April 12, 1901, Rockhill Papers.

mand punishment of the guilty, and secure posthumous honors for the Chinese officials who had lost their lives in opposing the Boxers.[31]

The amount of the money indemnity was the major question facing the powers in the negotiations. Rockhill believed that Germany, Russia, and France were intent on collecting an indemnity which would eventually impair China's independence. With the support of the Secretary of State, Conger and Rockhill advocated the adoption of a lump sum not to exceed $200,000,000, a figure considered to be within China's ability to pay.[32] Rockhill proposed that the lump sum be divided among the powers according to the percentage of the total loss each had suffered.

Of the other governments, Japan alone accepted the American proposal in its entirety.[33] The others accepted the lump sum principle but insisted on increasing the figure by two-thirds. Rockhill opposed the high indemnity until late in May, when the Chinese government issued an edict stating its willingness to pay $333,000,000, the sum set by a majority of the powers in the conference. Although he thought the indemnity exceeded either a reasonable assessment of the losses sustained or what China was able to pay, he realized that the amount was much less than it would have been had each nation submitted its claims separately. By its stand, the United States had saved China millions of dollars.

The action of Great Britain furnished Rockhill a lesson in diplomacy. The United States and Great Britain had a common policy in the Open Door. Moreover, Sir Ernest Satow, the British Minister, was a frequent guest in the Rockhill home, and often joined the Rockhills in their customary afternoon walks. But in the Peking negotiations, Great Britain was a poor diplomatic ally. She voted with Germany and Italy against Rockhill's amendment that each nation submit one claim to the Conference of Ministers rather than three categories of claims.[34] It was the first, but not the only, occasion on which Great Britain sided with Germany, a country which Rockhill found uncompromising in its indemnity demands. In April, Satow told Rockhill that his government favored scaling down the indemnity by approximately $37,000,000. Within a few days, however, to Rockhill's great amazement, the British came out in favor of the original sum. According to Rockhill, Great Britain made a concession to Germany at the last moment because of fear that she might join Russia and France in insisting on a guaranteed loan.[35] Thus, the relations of the European nations helped shape decisions in Peking.

The question of how the indemnity was to be paid was one of paramount importance. Three methods of payment were discussed. The floating of an international loan by China without a joint guarantee by the powers was dismissed

[31] *Foreign Relations: 1900*, pp. 219-20.

[32] *Foreign Relations: 1901*, Appendix, pp. 5-6.

[33] *Ibid.*, p. 87.

[34] *Ibid.*, p. 108.

[35] *Ibid.*, p. 171.

as too costly. Russia and France advocated a joint guarantee by the powers; the United States and Great Britain opposed this because a joint guarantee would lead to foreign intervention, if China should prove unable to meet the payments.[36] Rockhill sought to carry out Hay's instruction that the indemnity should be paid in bonds issued at par and bearing 3 per cent interest. The American proposal was finally adopted, but the interest rate was set at 5 per cent rather than 3 per cent as a concession to the Japanese, who claimed the increased rate necessary if Japan was not to sustain a loss on the bonds. Rockhill felt that the Japanese claim was just, and gave it his support. He wrote to Hay: "The embarrassment of Japan is so real, and on the other hand, that country deserves so much the thanks of all the others for the prompt, efficient, and modest, way in which it performed its work here last year, that I trust some means may be devised to prevent it sustaining any loss." [37]

Rockhill stood almost alone in fighting for the improvement of the conditions of foreign trade. He opposed the increased tariff rate which the other negotiators were willing to concede to China. The tariff increase was to provide a means of paying the indemnity until China granted some commercial concessions, such as the abolition of *likin,* an internal tax on trade.[38] Russia, France, and Germany, countries more interested in territorial acquisitions than in the China market, were opposed to making the higher tariff contingent upon China's granting of increased trade privileges.[39] The Japanese Minister originally supported Rockhill's views, but in June he, too, gave way, leaving Rockhill alone in his opposition to the raising of the tariff.[40] Again, Great Britain failed to support the American position, although her vast commercial interests would have benefited by the adoption of Rockhill's proposals. Rockhill attributed Great Britain's action to her desire to maintain close relations with Germany.

> The position of Germany on the question of the indemnity has, as I have advised you repeatedly, been most uncompromising. The urgent necessity for Great Britain to maintain her entente with Germany in China is, of course, responsible for the numerous concessions she has recently made to German insistence on being paid the last cent of her expenses. The most remarkable of these concessions is found, however, in the British Government's willingness to have the tariff on imports raised to an effective 5 per cent ad valorem, without compensating commercial advantages.[41]

Rockhill's aim was to strengthen China. Only if China could discharge her obligations and preserve her sovereignty could the United States hope to enjoy equality of commercial opportunity. This was the reason for his opposition to the levying of a large indemnity. It was also his reason for opposing the razing of Chinese forts, a question which provoked much difference of opinion in the

[36] *Ibid.,* p. 145.

[37] *Ibid.,* p. 245.

[38] *Ibid.,* pp. 227-30.

[39] *Ibid.,* p. 169.

[40] *Ibid.,* p. 227.

[41] *Ibid.,* p. 175.

conference. Rockhill argued that China must not be denied the means of protecting herself in the future, and that the forts represented no threat during the military occupation, for they could easily be taken over by the foreign troops.[42] For some time, Japan supported Rockhill on this question. When she finally agreed to the razing of the forts, Rockhill felt compelled to yield.[43] He was more successful in his opposition to the proposed prohibition on imports of armaments; the matter of enforcement was left finally to China.[44] In the matter of the treatment of the leaders of the Boxer revolt, the final decision to have China punish the guilty can be attributed, in large part, to Rockhill's efforts. Of the ten originally sentenced to death, Rockhill held that only four were guilty, and he was successful in his efforts to spare the lives of the innocent.[45]

The venture of the United States into world politics, via the Peking Conference of Ministers, tested American willingness to pay the price of influencing diplomatic affairs. The American government had not hesitated to send troops when the lives of Americans were in danger but it was quite another matter to maintain a military force at Peking primarily for the purpose of retaining a voice in the ensuing diplomatic negotiations. As early as September, 1900, President McKinley, probably mindful of the coming election, was of the opinion that American soldiers must be evacuated. John Hay and Alvey Adee did not share the President's view. Rockhill, too, urged that the American military force remain.[46] But, in March, 1901, General Chaffee, American commanding officer, told Rockhill that he had received orders to begin withdrawing his troops. Rockhill protested that such a withdrawal would mean the complete loss of influence in the diplomatic negotiations at a time when the most important questions remained undecided.[47]

The protocol signed at Peking on September 7, 1901, fell far short of the aims of Hay and Rockhill. Rockhill acknowledged, in his report to the Secretary of State, that the United States had at best succeeded only in preventing harsher terms being imposed. It was obvious that the struggle in China was only a lesser arena for the Western nations engaged in the diplomatic contest in Europe. Not long before the lengthy negotiations came to a close Rockhill wrote:

> I am sick and tired of the whole business and heartily glad to get away from it. I have been able to do something for commercial interests, and in a number of points have been able to carry out the Secretary's views, but have been practically alone in the negotiations. England has her agreement with Germany, Russia has her alliance with France, the Triple Alliance comes in here, and every other combina-

[42] *Ibid.*, p. 132.

[43] *Ibid.*, pp. 137-39.

[44] *Ibid.*, p. 297.

[45] *Ibid.*, pp. 5, 94-95.

[46] McKinley to Hay, September 14, 1900, Hay Papers.

[47] *Foreign Relations: 1901*, Appendix, pp. 110-11.

tion you know of is working here as it is in Europe. I trust it may be a long time before the United States gets into another muddle of this description.[48]

Unwilling to be more than a spectator of the struggle in Europe, the United States had less bargaining power in winning support for its aims in China.

When the Boxer Protocol was signed, the powers failed to foresee a decline in the value of the Chinese unit of currency. The sharp decline of the Chinese *tael* in 1902 led the powers, with the exception of the United States, to demand that China pay the equivalent of the value of the *tael* at the time the protocol was signed. In a memorandum for Hay, Rockhill concluded that the diplomats had never planned on an adjusted rate in the event of a fall in the exchange rate of the *tael,* nor had the Chinese so understood.[49] Rockhill's conclusions became the official position of the United States. So strongly did he feel about the demands of the other powers that he advised the Chinese Minister in Washington, Wu Ting-fang, that China should refer the question to the Hague Court, and that the United States would support China in her stand.[50] He also spoke to the German Ambassador in Washington, seeking to impress upon him the arbitrariness of the demands.[51] Rockhill's arguments failed to gain support. Conger, who had returned to Peking, reported the Russian and German ministers as saying that if one power wished to grant favors to China, it concerned that power only and the others would reserve their right of action.[52]

China was forced to pay additional *taels* as the exchange rate of the Chinese unit of currency declined. Hippisley wrote, early in 1903, that China was having to make an annual payment of 53.5 million *taels* instead of the 42.5 million originally agreed upon.[53]

Rockhill was convinced that an injustice was being perpetrated against China, but his influence on the negotiations was limited. He ably represented the interests of the United States and showed a strong desire to help China. At the opening of negotiations there was reason to believe that he would have the support of both Great Britain and Japan, nations whose policies were similar to those of the United States. This hope proved illusory. With Great Britain primarily concerned with her position in Europe, she paid more attention to the wishes of Germany than she did to her own interests in China. Japan did support the United States, but usually gave way before the demands of the majority. Thus, Rockhill found himself isolated. In spite of this handicap he did succeed in mitigating the harsh demands which would have been made had not the United States intervened. A few years later it was Rockhill who was

[48] Rockhill to Hippisley, July 6, 1901, Rockhill Papers.

[49] Rockhill to Hay, June 27, 1902, Rockhill Papers.

[50] Rockhill to Hippisley, August 16, 1902, Rockhill Papers.

[51] Speck von Sternburg to Rockhill, July 18, 1903, Rockhill Papers.

[52] Alvey A. Adee to Rockhill, July 9, 1902, Rockhill Papers.

[53] Hippisley to Rockhill, January 30, 1903, Rockhill Papers.

chiefly responsible for the return of the indemnity to China by the United States. Other nations eventually followed the example of this country, but the damage had been done. The settlement of 1901 imposed a heavy burden on the Chinese-Manchu government and contributed in a minor degree to the final fall of the Manchu dynasty, and the long series of civil wars which have wreaked havoc in China ever since.

CHAPTER SIX

A Lesson in Russian Mendacity

While her husband labored to bring about a better order in China, Edith found the role of diplomat's wife delightful. The dinners, the teas, the military reviews, the pony rides into the country, the afternoon walks, and the badminton games—even Will joined in the games—all gave her pleasure. The behavior of the American soldiers gained her praise, and she wrote in a tone of pride of the petition signed by five thousand Chinese asking that the American troops not be withdrawn. "Our men are certainly fine fellows, and way beyond the average of all the other armies." She had once reported, however, that their frequent drunkenness somewhat spoiled the effect of their honesty. She was proud of Will, too. "Will has had nothing but praise on all sides—he has been very successful in everything he has attempted to do, and though we have not gotten all we wanted, we have vastly more than ever seemed possible."

The days of August, 1901, dragged on interminably. Peking was surprisingly cool after the sizzling days of July, but now that the time had arrived to leave, beautiful Litchfield in the Connecticut Berkshires held more inviting charm than the ancient Manchu-Chinese capital. The final departure was postponed repeatedly; Edith declared that "there [were] more objections to every step, than there [were] steps." She commented impatiently: "Great Britain is turning things over in her mighty mind and everyone is getting discouraged." Plans were made to sail on the *Empress of India* on September 5, but they had to be cancelled when the German Kaiser held up the final signing by insisting that the Chinese perform the kowtow before German dignitaries, a reversal of the ancient practice of prostrating oneself before the Emperor of China. Edith remarked: "It has been a funny game—has ended in the complete victory of the Chinese, much to everyone's delight, as the demand was too outrageous coming from a civilized Power—one who has always objected to the Kowtow."

Finally, on September 8, the Rockhills left Peking. "All the world came to the station to bid us bon voyage," Edith observed with pleasure. At Tientsin they spent three days waiting for a steamer. The waiting-time was brightened by dinner with Colonel Bower, the Tibetan explorer; a luncheon given by Mrs. Charles Denby; and another dinner in the Rockhills' honor by the British Consul-General. Edith, apologetic about the one evening dress she had with her, took comfort in the fact that since she was the only woman present at the dinners there was no way of making comparison.

Shocking news awaited the Rockhills at Shanghai. All flags were at half-mast as they came up the river. President William McKinley had succumbed to the wounds inflicted by an assassin. At the memorial service the following day in Shanghai, officers and sailors from the ships of several nations and the entire consular body attended.

Thus, when the Rockhills sailed for home, Theodore Roosevelt, a long-time friend and admirer, had been elevated to the Presidency. Rockhill was Roosevelt's oracle on Far Eastern questions. Two years later, when the Minister to Korea, Horace Allen, returned to the United States full of the fears aroused by the aggressive Japanese, the President advised him "to tell Rockhill everything and he would dole it out to him [Roosevelt] as he could use it." [1] In the same conversation, Roosevelt spoke of Rockhill as "the author and sponsor of our Asiatic policy." [2] Roosevelt later ranked Rockhill as one of the three men in the foreign service who had been most valuable to him.

Resuming his duties as Director of the Bureau of American Affairs and as Far Eastern adviser to the Department of State upon his return to Washington, Rockhill was very much in the sun as the trusted and admired friend of both the President and Secretary Hay. Enjoying the complete confidence of his superiors, Rockhill served as a one-man Far Eastern divison at a time when that office had yet to be established.

From Peking, Rockhill had seen Russia sweep down over Manchuria when the Boxers destroyed Russian property. Seeing in the insurrection an unprecedented opportunity for seizing control of all Manchuria, the Russians had quickly extended operations beyond the railway zone where they enjoyed a treaty right to station guards. By October, 1900, they had taken full possession of Mukden, Newchwang, and the railroad as far south as Tientsin. Russian policy clearly called for adding Manchuria to her Siberian maritime provinces. Rockhill had returned to Washington overwhelmingly convinced that Russia was determined to acquire as much of China as possible.

To contain Czarist imperialism in the Far East, Rockhill had to rely largely on verbal protests. Secretary Hay told Roosevelt: "I take it for granted that Russia knows as well as we do that we will not fight over Manchuria, for the simple reason that we cannot. . . . If our rights and our interests in opposition to Russia in the Far East were as clear as noonday, we could never get a treaty through the Senate the object of which was to check Russian aggression." [3]

Rockhill could count on Japan and Great Britain to resist the Russian advance. In 1902 these two nations had joined in an alliance directed at Russia. While the United States had a mutual interest with them, Rockhill had to

---

[1] Horace Allen to E. V. Morgan, March 6, 1903, Allen Manuscripts, New York Public Library; cited by Fred Harvey Harrington, *God, Mammon and the Japanese* (Madison: University of Wisconsin Press, 1944), p. 314.

[2] Allen to Rockhill, January 4, 1904, Allen Manuscripts, New York Public Library; cited by Harrington, *ibid.*

[3] Secretary of State John Hay to President Theodore Roosevelt, April 28, 1903, Hay Papers.

act as if the United States had no more in common with them than she did with Russia. The only course open was one of independent action and this Rockhill pursued.

Convinced of the importance of halting Russian expansion, Rockhill sought to do so under Article XI of the Boxer Protocol, which provided for the revision of commercial treaties with China.[4] In drafting the treaty, Rockhill's aims were more political than commercial. Seeking to weaken the hold of the Czar's government, Rockhill asked China to open to foreign trade two localities in the heart of the area, now occupied by Russian troops and governed by Russian officials.

Rockhill learned in April, 1903, that the Czar's government, in opposing China's consideration of the American proposal, was resorting to threats. Russia made evacuation of Manchuria contingent upon China's refusal to open any new cities to trade and upon an agreement not to employ any foreigners in her service other than Russians.[5] This word was confidentially communicated by the Japanese Legation in Washington and by Minister Conger in Peking. Armed with this information, Hay had a long conversation with Cassini, the Russian Ambassador in Washington. Hay reported to Roosevelt: "He pretended to know nothing whatever about the convention, but discussed it point by point in a manner as clear and minute as if he had written it himself." [6] On April 29, Hay received a message from the American Ambassador at St. Petersburg, who had been instructed to make inquiries, that Foreign Minister Lamsdorf denied all knowledge of any Russian demands on China. The very next day Conger cabled that the Russian Chargé d'Affaires had repeated the demands on China. Hay confessed that "dealing with a government with whom mendacity is a science is an extremely difficult and delicate matter" but thought that St. Petersburg might, in the face of opposition, repudiate the Chargé d'Affaires at

[4] Article XI of the Boxer Protocol provided for the revision of commercial treaties. Rockhill had advocated that the nations represented in the Conference of Ministers proceed jointly in revising the treaties. The representatives of the other powers did not agree. Had joint negotiations been instituted, it is possible that the system of internal taxation known as *likin* would have been abolished—which was one of Rockhill's chief aims. *Likin* was a duty levied on goods in transit from one province to another. Foreign goods were exempt from this tax upon payment at the port of entry of a commutation transit tax of two and one-half per cent, but they were still subject to examination causing delay. China was willing to abolish *likin* in return for a ten per cent tariff. Great Britain insisted on complete abolition, a demand which Rockhill considered unreasonable and to which China would not agree. Rockhill wrote: "Most of the obstacles of trade, of which the Americans as well as other foreign merchants in China complain, are so intimately connected with the question of inland taxation that unless some method can be devised for either abolishing the inland tax or regulating it more satisfactorily than at present, it seems to me improbable that any great results can be expected from a revision of our commercial treaties." *Foreign Relations: 1901,* Appendix, p. 252.

[5] *Foreign Relations: 1903,* p. 53.

[6] Hay to Roosevelt, April 28, 1903, Hay Papers.

Peking.[7] If this turned out to be correct, Hay was willing to forget the Russian's subterfuge. "We are not charged with the cure of the Russian soul, and we may let them go to the devil at their own sweet will."

Rockhill proposed that the disclaimer of opposition to the opening of Manchurian ports by the Russian Foreign Minister be tested. He drafted an instruction to the American treaty commissioners, who were negotiating with the Chinese at Shanghai, directing them to present the Chinese with the Russian denial. Rockhill hoped that the Chinese would take courage and comply with the American request, but, on May 18, the American commissioners cabled that China still refused to open the localities in Manchuria. Again, on May 29, China notified Conger that the Russian Chargé d'Affaires had reiterated his demands and that China could not conveniently agree to the opening of the Manchurian ports in the commercial treaty.[8] Russia, in spite of her statement on April 29, continued to exert pressure on China.

When China continued to refuse on the grounds that Russia was fighting the proposal, the United States sought the aid of the Russian Minister in Peking.[9] This move resulted in a new series of Russian diplomatic gyrations designed to avoid offending the United States while opposing American aims in regard to Manchuria. The Russian Minister in Peking, Pavel Lessar, advised Minister Conger that he could not cooperate without instructions from his government. Early in June, Secretary Hay advised Conger that the matter of cooperation had been referred to Cassini, the Russian Ambassador in Washington.[10] Two weeks later, Conger was told that the Russians requested that he (Conger) communicate to the Russian Minister at Peking the demands of the United States.[11] But when Conger and Lessar conferred, the Russian declared that he had no instructions except to await discussion of the question in Washington.[12] Finally, on July 14, the persistence of Hay and Rockhill was rewarded. The Russian Chargé d'Affaires handed to Hay a statement that Russia had withdrawn her objections. A copy was immediately dispatched to Conger.[13]

The Russian statement did not entirely clear the way: Prince Ch'ing, head

[7] Hay to Roosevelt, May 12, 1903, Hay Papers.

[8] Draft of Instruction to Conger, May 29, 1903, Rockhill Papers.

The apparent inconsistency of Russian replies to American inquiries was due to a sharp conflict at St. Petersburg between the Ministers of Foreign Affairs and Finance who favored peaceful economic penetration and the Minister of War who advocated use of force. In 1903 this struggle was further complicated by the strong influence on the Czar of "Bezobrazov's Circle." For the story of Captain Bezobrazov and his expansionist projects in the Far East, see David S. Crist, "Russia's Far Eastern Policy In The Making," *Journal of Modern History,* XIV, September, 1942, pp. 317-41.

[9] *Foreign Relations: 1903,* p. 60.

[10] *Ibid.,* p. 63.

[11] *Ibid.,* p. 64.

[12] *Ibid.,* p. 65.

[13] *Ibid.,* p. 67.

of the Chinese Foreign Office, replied that the Russians had not intimated withdrawal of their demands, and that, as long as Russia occupied Manchuria, China could not open the localities. He did, however, present a written promise to Minister Conger that China would open two ports to foreign trade, by imperial edict, when the Russian evacuation had been completed.[14] This fell short of American demands, since it indefinitely postponed the opening of ports by making it subject to Russian evacuation and by failure to agree to provide for the opening in the commercial treaty. Conger telegraphed that he thought this was the best that China could do and the treaty ought to be concluded immediately without provision regarding the opening of ports.[15]

Rockhill was not pleased with Conger's proposed concessions to China. He postponed a planned trip to Europe. "If things go badly, I will stay here until they are settled. I need not leave here until the 18th. of August. I do not feel that I would enjoy my holiday with all this uncertainty about the Chinese matter." [16]

Rockhill drafted new instructions for Conger, which he hoped would "ginger him up," [17] and sent the draft to Hay, who was at his summer home in New Hampshire, for approval. The instruction sent to Conger on July 26 was identical in substance with Rockhill's draft. Conger was to insist that the opening of Mukden and Tatung Kun be provided in the treaty, to state that the United States would wait until October 8 for the signing of the treaty; and to add that the ports should be opened no later than three months after the treaty was signed.[18]

Fearful that there might be misunderstanding, Rockhill called on Wu Tingfang, the Chinese Minister in Washington, on the last Saturday in July. He informed the Minister of the new policy, and told him that what the United States asked "was in the interest of China, more in fact than in that of the United States. . . ." To Hay he confided: "I think there is no doubt that while the Russians have officially informed you that they have absolutely no objection to the Chinese opening new localities to trade, they are working against it in every way they possibly can, and have so intimidated Prince Ching that he does not dare do it." [19]

While Rockhill and Hay were intent on calling Russia's hand, they did not excuse the Chinese. The Secretary of State was annoyed by the Chinese and re-

---

[14] *Ibid.,* pp. 68-69.

[15] *Ibid.,* p. 68.

[16] Rockhill to Hay, July 23, 1903, Rockhill Papers.

[17] *Ibid.*

[18] The date set for the signing of the treaty, October 8, 1903, was also the date set for the final evacuation of Russian troops in the agreement of April 8, 1902. Rockhill's unwillingness to accept the Chinese proposal that the opening of ports be contingent upon Russian evacuation makes it clear that he did not expect the Russians to adhere to the agreement. Rockhill's draft of the instruction to Conger is in the Rockhill Papers. A paraphrase of the instruction is given in *Foreign Relations: 1903,* p. 70.

[19] Rockhill to Hay, August 3, 1903, Rockhill Papers.

ferred to them as being false and timid. He wrote: "We have done the Chinks a great service, which they don't seem inclined to recognize. It will never do to let them imagine they can treat us as they please, and that the only power they need fear is Russia." [20] Rockhill, too, was irritated by the dilatoriness of the Chinese. But the hesitation of the Manchu-Chinese was understandable in view of the occupation of Manchuria by Russian troops and the inclination of the Russians to find a pretext for the annexation of territory.

On August 13, Prince Ch'ing agreed to the American demands and the treaty was signed on October 8. Speck von Sternburg, German Ambassador in Washington, complimented Rockhill on achieving "a most extraordinary diplomatic success." [21]

While Secretary Hay has received the credit for the victory, it was Rockhill who carried on the negotiations. He had almost a free hand, thanks to Hay's complete faith in his ability. The Rockhill-Hay correspondence during the summer of 1903 offers abundant evidence of the close personal ties existing between the two men. Hay made only the most minor changes in the many instructions drafted by Rockhill, and at one point Hay was admittedly confused in regard to important details as a result of his having left the negotiations so completely in the hands of his Far Eastern adviser.[22] When Rockhill stopped in Newport early in August, the Secretary wrote a friendly letter extending an invitation to visit "our shanty." [23] In the middle of August, Rockhill left for Europe, but he returned to Washington before the end of September. Hay wrote that Rockhill's presence was a comfort to Adee and would be to him when he returned to Washington.[24]

The signing of the Chinese treaty did not guarantee the Open Door to American trade in Manchuria. Rockhill continued to view Russia as the power to be feared, and, on October 28, prepared the draft of a dispatch to be forwarded to the Foreign Office in St. Petersburg offering the assistance of the United States in bringing about a settlement of the questions pending between that country and China. It is unlikely, however, that such a dispatch was sent.[25]

In December the Department of State received a report from Henry Miller,

---

[20] Hay to Rockhill, July 24, 1903, Rockhill Papers.

[21] Sternburg to Rockhill, July 18, 1903, Rockhill Papers.

[22] On July 31, 1903, Hay wrote to Rockhill: "One thing lacks clearness, to my mind. Are we asking Ching to sign a separate article on Manchurian ports Oct. 8, or an engagement to sign the Commercial Treaty, including that clause Oct. 8?" On July 26 a telegram, drafted by Rockhill but sent out under Hay's name, demanded that Prince Ch'ing sign a note agreeing to sign the treaty on October 8. *Foreign Relations: 1903,* p. 70. Hay's letter to Rockhill, July 31, 1903, is among the Rockhill Papers.

[23] Hay to Rockhill, August 12, 1903, Rockhill Papers.

[24] Hay to Rockhill, September 20, 1903, Rockhill Papers.

[25] Draft of Instructions to the United States Ambassador to Russia, October 28, 1903, Rockhill Papers.

Examination of the dispatches in the Department of State Archives failed to reveal instruction to the United States Ambassador to Russia along the lines of this draft.

American Consul at Newchwang, citing Russian discriminations against American commerce in Manchuria. Rockhill, impressed by the evidence, suggested that the matter be brought to the attention of the Russian government, and in a memorandum to Hay, he cited many reports received during the year complaining of Russian violations of the Open Door. The Russians made it difficult for Americans to ship their goods to the interior over Russian railroads, levied discriminatory rates, exacted unwarranted fees, and at Dalny made it impossible for Americans to secure suitable locations for business. As a possible course of action, Rockhill advised:

> Although I fancy that the Russian Government will for a long time to come insist that conditions are not yet such in Manchuria, as to enable it to regulate railroad rates and grant our people the rights which we are undoubtedly entitled to in Manchuria, nevertheless, it seems to me that it is very nearly high time to bring the matter to the attention of the Russian Government. I don't think that we can secure what Consular [*sic*] Miller suggests in this dispatch—"the same liberty and rights that Russian subjects enjoy in our country"—but I certainly think it may be possible, by tactful representations at St. Petersburg, to secure serious consideration of the perfectly arbitrary and unjustifiable efforts of the Russian authorities in Manchuria to exclude us from the markets there.
>
> We might start in, at all events, and work up the case with such documents as we have, and see if we can make it sufficiently strong for our purpose, and if not, I do not doubt that we can promptly secure from our consular officer and the American business houses there all the necessary data.[26]

While Rockhill's suggestions had not been acted upon before the outbreak of war in February, 1904, the Department of State remained firm in its stand. As late as January 20, Secretary Hay called the attention of the Russian Ambassador, Count Cassini, to a newspaper item in which it was reported that a Russian official in the Far East had called the American commercial treaty with China "unfriendly and undiplomatic." [27] The same official was also quoted as saying that Russia would not open consulates at Mukden and Antung, nor would she allow other nations to do so. United States Ambassador McCormick, at St. Petersburg, was furnished a copy of Hay's note and instructed to make such use of it as he deemed "expedient and fit." [28]

Russian expansion posed the most serious threat to American interests in the Far East during the period from the Sino-Japanese War of 1894-1895 to the Russo-Japanese War of 1904-1905. Russian aims and actions were openly aggressive. When St. Petersburg sought to veil her expansionist policy with repeated avowals of peaceful intentions and with public statements in support of China's territorial and administrative integrity, Americans could only con-

[26] Rockhill memorandum to Hay, December 24, 1903, Rockhill Papers.

[27] Hay to Count Arthur Cassini, January 20, 1904, Department of State Archives.

[28] Francis B. Loomis to Robert S. McCormick, January 22, 1904, Department of State Archives.

clude that Russian diplomacy was guilty of aggressiveness and deceit. Their contemporary experiences with Japan on the other hand caused them to believe that the United States and Japan had common aims. Rockhill was friendly to the Japanese. He had kept Takahira, Japan's Ambassador in Washington, informed during the course of the negotiations of the commercial treaty with China in 1903, and had solicited his views on various measures.[29]

When the Russo-Japanese War broke out in February, 1904, Rockhill was strongly anti-Russian and pro-Japanese. To his friend, Horace Allen, Minister to Korea, who favored American support of Korean independence, he wrote that he saw no possibility of the United States assuming the role of protector of Korea. Korea would be taken care of by Japan when the war was over, and he gave his approval of this solution to the Korean problem. "The annexation of Korea to Japan seems to me absolutely indicated as the one great and final step westward to the extension of the Japanese Empire. I think when this comes about it will be better for the Korean people and also for the peace in the Far East." [30] Rockhill was amused by the spectacle of the Japanese escorting the Russian Minister and his legation guard out of Seoul. When a friend in Boston wrote to Rockhill that the American Asiatic Association was blindly partisan to Japan and failed to view the Far Eastern scene from an American point of view, Rockhill took occasion to assail the Russians. The Bostonian noted the historic friendship of the United States and Russia. Rockhill, cynically objective, replied:

> I must say that I don't attach much importance to the question of Russian friendship in 1863. Gratitude between nations is a poor thing to count on where material interests do not come in to strengthen it and keep it alive. We can still stand a certain amount of gratitude to France, but trade and a certain similarity in our views on many subjects make it endurable. I don't see that the same reasons exist in the case of Russia. I don't think there is a nation on the face of the earth which has fewer points of contact, intellectually or in any other shape, with us than it.[31]

In a letter to Edwin Denby, son of the former Minister to China, he expressed the opinion that the feeling against Russia among Americans was "due entirely to the disingenuous and shifty methods of the Russian Foreign Office and its agents in the last five or six years." He thought it was fortunate "that some nation is willing to risk all that it has to secure from them guarantees sufficient to restrain them, and thereby contribute to insure the peace of that part of the world." [32] Rockhill's admiration of the Japanese was, perhaps, the weakest point in his diplomatic armor.

With the Japanese attack on the Russian fleet on February 8, the greatest

[29] D. W. Stevens, adviser to Japanese Legation in Washington, to Rockhill, August 8, 1903, Rockhill Papers.

[30] Rockhill to Allen, February 20, 1904, Rockhill Papers.

[31] Rockhill to F. B. Forbes, March 9, 1904, Rockhill Papers.

[32] Rockhill to Edwin Denby, March 19, 1904, Rockhill Papers.

danger confronting the United States was the possible spread of hostilities to China. A German proposal asking that the President send a circular note to the belligerents calling on them to observe the neutrality of China was forwarded to Rockhill by the President.

Rockhill advised the President that the proposal "might also be interpreted as a tacit acknowledgment of the right of Russia to continue in military occupation of Manchuria, an integral part of the Chinese Empire, against which occupation the Chinese government has made and is still making a constant protest." He thought that the German neutralization plan was additionally dangerous in that it called for occupation of China by foreign troops. The presence of foreign troops would probably create unrest among the people and cause the Emperor to flee. Rockhill continued: "I should have mentioned that if the German suggestion were carried out, it might prove highly prejudicial to Japan's interests, for by the neutralization of China that country would be precluded from joining forces with Japan at some time during the coming struggle, when her aid might bring about the final defeat of Russia." [33]

Though Rockhill saw many objections to the Kaiser's suggestion, Roosevelt approved the sending of a circular note to Great Britain, France, and Germany to request the belligerents to respect the neutrality of China and, in all practicable ways, her administrative entity.[34] This differed from the German proposal which asked that the belligerents "respect the neutrality of China outside the sphere of military action." This clause would have given Russia a free hand north of the Great Wall.

[33] Rockhill memorandum to Roosevelt, February 6, 1904, Roosevelt Papers, Library of Congress.

[34] *Foreign Relations: 1904,* p. 327.

CHAPTER SEVEN

Standing at the Right Hand of Roosevelt

In 1904, Theodore Roosevelt was elected to the Presidency, the office which had come to him in 1901 as a result of an assassin's bullet. In accordance with newspaper rumors during the campaign, Roosevelt, in December, named Rockhill as Conger's successor at the Court in Peking. In January, Rockhill made a hurried trip to Europe to visit his mother and to bring his daughter, Margarita, who had been attending a private school in Switzerland, back to the United States. In April the Rockhills sailed for China. On June 1, 1905, he officially took over his duties as Minister.

When the Rockhills arrived, a new Legation building was under construction—a poorly designed structure reflecting the American architect's specialization in post offices. With columns of tin and only one balcony, although the extreme heat of Peking summers made it desirable to have several, the new building would have been much more in harmony with surroundings in Chicago than in Peking. But it could have evoked aesthetic appreciation in neither. It was, said Rockhill, "a terrible blot on the landscape." However, the new Minister had a free hand in the purchase of furnishings and here he indulged his taste for things Chinese.

During the construction of the new Legation the Rockhills lived in the renovated temple which the Congers had occupied. It was wholly inadequate for entertaining visitors, and the Rockhills worried about the projected visit of Alice Roosevelt, the President's daughter. Her father was sending her with the Secretary of War, William Howard Taft, on a trip to Japan, the Philippines, and China. The party was a large one including a group of senators, representatives, other notables of Washington officialdom, and a considerable number of newspapermen. To accommodate this throng in Peking, with only a temporary Legation building and one first-class hotel, without leaving any one disgruntled, seemed impossible. Rockhill wrote to the President expressing his delight at the prospect of seeing Miss Roosevelt and stating his regret that the new Legation would not be ready. At present, he wrote, we are "camping in some old Chinese houses." Fortunately, Secretary Taft and several others returned to the United States from Canton without seeing Peking, but even so, the problem was not solved. When the party arrived in September, members of the press complained bitterly because they had to go to third-rate hotels.

Alice, amazed by the great new world of Peking, seems to have been pleased by the reception tendered her. After spending the first night in the Legation, Alice, the Rockhills, and some of the more prominent members of the party were guests at the summer palace of the Empress Dowager. On the third day, at eight o'clock in the morning, the audience with the Empress Dowager took place and Mrs. Rockhill presented Alice. While talking to the Empress Dowager in the gardens, Alice was given an exhibition of the choleric disposition of the "Old Buddha," who turned suddenly on the former Minister to the United States, Wu Ting-fang. What he had done to infuriate Her Majesty, if anything, Alice did not know but she saw him turn "quite gray," and he "got down on all fours, his forehead touching the ground." Alice thought the Empress might at any moment say, "Off with his head."

Alice's only complaint concerning her stay in Peking was that she did not have time to see all the sights. Lesser members of the party were bitter because Rockhill had not included them in the visit to the Court. A request that they be admitted would never have been granted. Rockhill wrote to James L. Rodgers, American Consul-General at Shanghai: "My experience with a section of the Taft party which came up here was identical with yours. I never saw such a pack of irresponsible men and women in my life. . . . Yesterday, at 11 A.M., I was glad to say goodby to the last of them at Tientsin." [1]

Yet Rockhill faced more serious problems. The immigration policy of the United States threatened to undo all that had been accomplished in strengthening the ties between the two countries. Since 1880, when she reluctantly agreed to a new treaty revising the policy of encouragement to Chinese immigration, China had looked with displeasure on the bars erected against her emigrants. Again in 1894, China had consented to a treaty embodying the policy of exclusion, but, when this treaty came up for renewal in 1904, she was adamant in her refusal to perpetuate what she considered an injustice. Before leaving Washington, Rockhill had carried on negotiations in the hope of bringing about a settlement.

If the government at Peking had any inclination to give in to the United States, the certainty of the sharp and dangerous criticism that would follow discouraged any such step. A young generation of students, who had studied abroad and who were deeply sensitive to the profound humiliation to which their country had been subjected, considered the American exclusion policy an unbearable insult. Choosing the boycott as one of the few weapons available to them, these students set out to force the United States to alter its policy. Provincial officials gave the anti-American movement their support partly because of sympathy with its objectives and partly because it furnished an opportunity to embarrass the Peking government. They disliked the Peking government because of its attempt to centralize political power in its own hands. Merchants, too, supported the agitation because of their sympathy with the Cantonese who suffered most directly by American exclusion.

The Chinese, hurt by the fact that they were singled out as undesirable immigrants, also protested against the unfair treatment of their fellow nationals in the United States. While the Chinese in the United States theoretically enjoyed the

[1] W. W. Rockhill to James L. Rodgers, September 18, 1905, Rockhill Papers.

same rights as citizens of the most favored nation, they were targets of disdain and racial animosity. Immigration officials showed little or no respect for the rights of Chinese. They were particularly harsh in enforcing the Geary Act of 1892 which placed upon the Chinese the burden of proof of their right to be in the United States. This act made it the duty of all Chinese laborers to obtain a certificate of residence; failure to do so resulted in deportation. Chinese found here illegally were subjected to a penalty of one year's imprisonment and then returned to China. Other grievances arose out of the inadequacies of an immigration system which permitted Chinese to make the long and expensive trip to the United States only to be rejected. In 1905, 25 per cent of those arriving were forced to return.

American statesmen recognized the causes for the Chinese complaints. Roosevelt wrote to Rockhill: "I am trying in every way to make things easy for the Chinese here. Chinese laborers must be kept out of this country, but I want to secure the best possible treatment for Chinese business men, students and travelers." [2] Secretary of War Taft likewise expressed sympathy with the Chinese. Speaking before the graduating class at Miami University in Ohio, Taft asked:

> Is it just that, for the purpose of excluding or preventing perhaps one hundred Chinese coolies from slipping into this country against the law, we should subject an equal number of Chinese merchants and students of high character to an examination of such an inquisitorial, humiliating, insulting, and physically uncomfortable character as to discourage altogether the coming of merchants and students? [3]

But while some national leaders took a sympathetic point of view, racial antagonism and economic self-interest had created a deep hostility toward the Chinese among the people in the Pacific coastal states and they were unyielding in their demands for exclusion. It was not only the hoodlums and hooligans who taunted the Chinese: even the more respectable members of society questioned whether Chinese immigrants were susceptible to the Americanizing processes. This hostile opinion on the West Coast could not be disregarded by political candidates no matter what their private feelings might be on the Chinese question. Candidates for national office felt the need of wooing the West-Coast electorate. This is evident in the fact that with one exception, all laws and treaties restricting Chinese immigration were enacted on the eve of national elections. Consequently, exclusion was a national policy and Minister Rockhill soon found himself in the unenviable position of attempting to reconcile the irreconcilable Chinese and Californians.

Yet, when Rockhill left Washington in April, 1905, he expected no great difficulty. The past failure of the Chinese to present a united front in behalf of any cause led responsible officials, including the newly appointed Minister,

[2] President Theodore Roosevelt to Rockhill, May 18, 1905, Rockhill Papers.

[3] *The Nation,* June 22, 1905, p. 491.

to believe that no serious controversy was imminent. He soon learned that he was mistaken.

A storm of anti-American protests greeted Rockhill on his arrival at Shanghai. At the great port city he saw hundreds of placards reminding the Chinese in angry terms of the ill treatment received by their fellow nationals in the United States, and in the native newspapers he read articles attacking the Americans and calling for a boycott of American goods. On his arrival in Peking numerous petitions awaited him, calling for redress in most serious terms. It was difficult to believe that the Chinese, so long accustomed to arbitrary treatment at the hands of the great powers, could muster up so much enthusiasm for a cause. But the American Consul, Rockhill's reliable friend Fleming Duncan Cheshire, who at first minimized the movement, advised him that the Chinese were "taking up the boycott heart and soul." [4]

Never given to alarm, Rockhill refused to dramatize the difficulties of his position just as he had refused to dramatize his early days in New Mexico or his hardships in Mongolia and Tibet, but bare facts concerning the movement were sufficient to arouse concern. While the boycott was restricted to the treaty ports, the inflammatory denunciation of Americans and the zeal of the supporters of the movement evoked memories of the Boxer revolt. At a meeting at Shanghai, on July 19, fifteen hundred attended, including students from twenty schools and delegates from the chambers of commerce and guilds of Shanghai, Canton, Fukien, Hankow, and Shantung. Speeches called for a firm front to show the world "that in this instance, at any rate, there is a united China," and everyone present agreed not to buy more American goods.[5] At Canton, where much discontent and considerable revolutionary activity prevailed, students distributed placards calling for support of the boycott while the native press denounced the United States. The American Consul at Canton reported heavy losses to American business firms; the Standard Oil Company alone claimed a loss of $25,000. Rockhill received telegrams and dispatches reporting that the movement had spread to Foochow, Amoy, Hankow, and Tientsin, but nothing had occurred at these places to cause apprehension.[6]

Although Roosevelt and Rockhill indicated a degree of sympathy with some of the objectives of the boycott, they could not condone it. Roosevelt, jittery about the threat to American commerce, wrote almost weekly letters to Rockhill. In an executive order on June 24, the President, seeking to alleviate some of the grievances of the Chinese, warned that Chinese eligible for admission must be accorded the same treatment as citizens of the most favored nation, and that immigration officials guilty of discourtesy or arbitrary treatment would be dis-

[4] Fleming Duncan Cheshire to Rockhill, June 23, 1905, Rockhill Papers.

[5] Rockhill to Secretary of State Elihu Root, July 26, 1905, Enclosure 1, Clipping from the *North China Daily News,* July 21, 1905, Department of State Archives.

[6] Rockhill to Root, August 17, 1905, Department of State Archives.

missed.[7] But on the question of admitting Chinese laborers, Roosevelt remained firm. Invoking his habitual moral tone, he proclaimed that "The greatest of all duties is national self-preservation, and the most important step in national self-preservation is to preserve in every way the well-being of the worker." [8] And exclusion of Chinese laborers, concluded the President, was necessary to the well-being of the American worker. To Rockhill he wrote: "I intend to do the Chinese justice and am taking a far stiffer tone with my own people than any President has ever yet taken, both about immigration, about this indemnity, and so forth. In return it is absolutely necessary for you to take a stiff tone with the Chinese when they are clearly in the wrong." [9] Having discharged his duty, insofar as he saw it, to do justice to the Chinese, Roosevelt was prepared to deal firmly with the Peking government and he expected Rockhill to do likewise.

Although beset by an impatient Chief Executive, nudged by business representatives in China—whom one consul described as "regular wild Indians" and as having "gone mad"—and confronted by a Manchu-Chinese government incapable of taking effective action, Rockhill retained the traditional calm of an old Buddha. From the beginning he believed that, while the situation was serious and might easily develop into an antiforeign movement of the proportions of 1900, the United States must be patient and refrain from threats of force. He understood, as did few others, that to force the government of China to take hasty measures might easily result in revolution and even greater losses to American merchants. While firm and persistent in dealing with China, he did his best to prevent his own government from taking precipitate action. On June 24, Rockhill wrote to Hay asking if he could agree that all Chinese proving to the satisfaction of the United States that they were not laborers would be admitted. This was a concession in that the treaty provided for admission of only students, merchants, travelers, and officials.[10] In July, while the anti-American movement was at its height, he wrote to Roosevelt concerning his discussions with Hay of a proposal to return the Boxer indemnity.[11] Even though Americans at home were becoming restive and those in China were alarmed, Rockhill took time to write to the State Department making objective comments on the boycott as a sign of the much-to-be-desired nationalism which would make China strong and able to stand on her own feet.[12]

During the early weeks of the boycott, Rockhill provided American consuls

[7] Rockhill to Root, August 29, 1905, Enclosure 2, Rockhill to Prince Ch'ing, August 27, 1905, Department of State Archives.

[8] Theodore Roosevelt's Speech at Atlanta, Georgia, *A Compilation of the Messages and Speeches of Theodore Roosevelt, 1901-1905,* ed. Alfred Henry Lewis (Washington: Bureau of National Literature and Art, 1905), p. 693.

[9] Roosevelt to Rockhill, August 22, 1905, Rockhill Papers.

[10] Rockhill to Secretary of State John Hay, June 17, 1905, Department of State Archives.

[11] Rockhill to Roosevelt, July 12, 1905, Rockhill Papers.

[12] Rockhill to Root, August 26, 1905, Department of State Archives.

with a series of reasonable arguments to be used in seeking to convince the Chinese that it was a mistake. Fearing that, in the tenseness of the crisis, consuls might resort to threats, he carefully instructed them to avoid doing so. At a later date, when the Consul at Canton, Julius Lay, cabled directly to Washington for a warship and his request was granted, Rockhill protested vigorously to Secretary of State Elihu Root. He told Root of the tendency among the young and inexperienced consuls to request the presence of a man-of-war when there was no necessity for it and warned him against a renewal of the old "gunboat policy." [13]

In his own dealings with the Peking government, Rockhill demanded that action be taken to suppress the anti-American agitation. He held that the boycott was an unfriendly act; that the movement grew out of the false allegation that the United States was trying to impose unfair demands on China; and that, while the United States could not consent to admitting Chinese laborers, it was willing to discuss other questions relating to Chinese immigration. In conferences with Prince Ch'ing, he insisted that local officials must be instructed to put an end to the movement, and he was sharp in his criticism of those who showed any sympathy with the boycott.

Rockhill's persistent calls at the Foreign Office brought only vague assurances that the government was taking action. However, the provincial officials, who continued in sympathy with the boycott, failed to lift a hand in opposition to the movement. Rockhill was not deceived and continued to press Prince Ch'ing for action. His belief that the Peking government had done nothing seemed confirmed when the Chinese Consul-General at San Francisco assured his fellow countrymen in California that the Foreign Office had informed him that "it had never at any time prohibited or obstructed the boycott." [14]

In August, Rockhill revised his tactics. He secured the consent of the State Department to two measures which ultimately proved effective.[15] First he informed the Foreign Office that the Imperial government would be held responsible for losses under Article XV of the Treaty of 1858.[16] Second, he refused to discuss the terms of the new treaty until the agitation had been suppressed.[17] In addition, he called for the deprivation of rank for Tseng Shao-ching, President of the Fu-kien merchants' guild and *taot'ai* in Shanghai.[18] He also cited President

[13] *Ibid.,* September 18, 1905.

[14] Alvey A. Adee to Rockhill, July 26, 1905, Department of State Archives.

[15] Rockhill to Root, August 4, 1905; Root to Rockhill, August 6, 1905; Rockhill to Root, August 27, 1905; Department of State Archives.

[16] Rockhill to Prince Ch'ing, August 7, 1905, Department of State Archives.

[17] Rockhill to Root, August 17, 1905, Enclosure 3, Rockhill to Prince Ch'ing, August 14, 1905, Department of State Archives.

[18] *Ibid.,* Enclosure 2, August 7, 1905.

Prince Ch'ing stated in his reply of August 29 that Tseng Shao-ching was merely a member of a commercial guild "and we cannot enlarge upon his offense and deal severely with him for fear of exciting still more trouble and disorder." Rockhill replied: "I urged

Roosevelt's order of June 24 as evidence that the United States government had gone as far as it could in meeting China's wishes until Congress should meet.[19] These steps, plus the changing attitude of the merchants as they began to lose money, caused the government of China to take more effective action against the boycott.

On August 17 the Senior Minister of the Foreign Office, H. E. Chu Hungch'i, called on the American Minister and told him that the provincial authorities had been ordered to stop the boycott.[20] He declared that Prince Ch'ing and the Grand Council were most anxious to stop the anti-American movement. Moreover, Rockhill was informed that proclamations by imperial order would be shortly put forth, but it was feared that to do so at once might lead to trouble. On August 26 Rockhill learned from Consul-General Rodgers at Shanghai that the *taot'ai* of the city had informed him that he would take immediate steps to end the agitation.[21] Rockhill's aims were further realized on August 31 with the issuance of an imperial edict condemning the boycott and declaring that viceroys and governors would be held responsible for its suppression.[22] Thus the government of China was publicly committed to bringing an end to the boycott.

In October, after the worst of the crisis had passed, Rockhill received a letter from Roosevelt concerning reports that the Japanese had encouraged the boycott. Rockhill's reply covered the whole subject of recent events in China in a thorough manner and with an insight reflecting his years of experience in the Orient. The letter to the President offered further evidence of Rockhill's refusal to accept hearsay, his insistence on investigating every aspect of a question before reaching a conclusion, and his complete integrity in stating what he believed to be the truth.

Regarding the role of the Japanese, Rockhill related how the American business men of Shanghai had blamed them, how he had carried on a careful investigation to determine the truth of the charges only to be forced to the conclusion that they were false, and how the Japanese in several treaty ports had cooperated in discouraging the boycott. He did not doubt that some Japanese had approved of it. He wrote:

> I do not of course think that all the Japanese, any more than all the British, German, Dutch, and Americans, even, have seen with disfavor this attempt on the part of the Chinese to coerce us. Many have found in it a source of profit;

on you his severe punishment, beginning with the deprivation of his official rank, because I was well aware that persons holding rank by purchase can be as readily punished for their offenses by their government as those holding substantive rank." Rockhill to Root, September 27, 1905, Enclosure 1, Rockhill to Prince Ch'ing, September 23, 1905; Department of State Archives.

[19] Rockhill to Root, August 29, 1905, Enclosure 2, Rockhill to Prince Ch'ing, August 27, 1905; Department of State Archives.

[20] Rockhill to Root, August 18, 1905, Department of State Archives.

[21] *Ibid.,* August 26, 1905.

[22] *Ibid.,* September 1, 1905.

others, Japanese, but especially Americans, thought—and may still think—it was and is an excellent plan to force on our country consideration of the rights of the Chinese and adoption of adequate measures to insure to the Chinese the enjoyment of them.[23]

In Rockhill's opinion, the boycott had first been suggested by the American press and "the movement in Shanghai was actually put in practical shape and started by two Americans. . . ." Rockhill further advised the President that the Manchu-Chinese officials had at first viewed the agitation with pleasure but when it threatened to become a widespread crusade against the foreigner they were frightened "and sought to stop the boycott, and to take out of the hands of the people a dangerous arm." But at that point, according to Rockhill, the government "found that it was exposing itself to seeing its orders disregarded, its prestige lessened, with no means of enforcing its commands, and that it was showing to its own people what all the rest of the world knows: that it is weak in means, weak in ability, weak especially in good able men." Not until the last day of August did the Peking government issue an imperial edict to stop the boycott, and even then it had to move cautiously, especially in the case of Canton where the Viceroy faced real dangers of revolution. With these considerations in mind Rockhill added: "I am fearful to force on such a weak Government the adoption of measures which would result, in all probability, in showing its weakness, when we want to make it stronger; of lessening its authority when we want to make it effective, so that it can discharge its international duties. The situation is, I admit, very embarrassing, and demands much patience." [24]

Having warned against forcing stronger measures on the debilitated and tottering Peking government, Rockhill advised: "I think it is my duty however to tell you that I firmly believe and I think all Americans out here agree with me, that if Congress at a very early date does not give some satisfaction to the legitimate complaints of the Chinese—or what they hold to be legitimate complaints—the boycott will revive throughout the Empire and do us irreparable harm." [25]

While the boycott was not a major problem of American diplomacy after August, it did not come to an end, and, as late as January, 1906, it continued a subject of diplomatic exchanges.

More significant, however, in the closing months of 1905 and the early part of 1906, were the reports of antiforeign disturbances and the rumors of continued agitation against Americans. When five missionaries were killed in October, 1905, in the so-called "Lienchou massacre," this seemed at first to be a part of the broad movement against Americans. The tragedy occurred in Kwangtung in the jurisdiction of the Liangkwang Viceroy, an official who had failed to take measures against the anti-American agitation. This fact Rockhill pointed out

[23] Rockhill to Roosevelt, October 30, 1905, Rockhill Papers.

[24] *Ibid.*

[25] *Ibid.*

to the Foreign Office.[26] Later investigation by American Consul Lay revealed that the outbreak resulted from the rivalry of Catholic and Protestant missionaries, and the antagonism aroused by the use of one of the native Chinese temples.[27] Deplorable as the massacre was, and though the government of China was responsible for the protection of missionaries, it was not an event to be interpreted as part of a vast antiforeign conspiracy. However, coming at a time when the boycott was still in progress—and in a province where the imperial edict of August 31 had been treated as waste paper—it is easy to understand why the event was given a broader significance than it deserved.

An event of major importance was the riot in the International Settlement at Shanghai on December 18. The riot was accompanied by a general strike organized by the leaders of the boycott. The disturbance led to the burning of the municipal police station and the freeing of prisoners. The German Consul and the American Vice-Consul were injured. American, British, German, Italian, and Japanese sailors were landed, and, with the aid of the volunteer corps, restored order.[28] Rockhill recommended that a warship be stationed at Shanghai for the protection of Americans but disagreed with the contention of James A. Jameson, President of the American Association of China, that the riot was the culmination of the boycott agitation.[29]

Rockhill later advised Secretary Root that the Shanghai riot was really the result of the unwise and unjustified policy of the British element in the International Settlement which wished to transform that area "into a republic on Chinese soil and under the protection of the guns of the Treaty Powers' ships." This policy, according to Rockhill, had never had the support of the British government.

> This pernicious activity at the present moment when the Chinese people are so keenly sensitive to every move of the foreigners which they think directly or indirectly conflicts with or tends to impair their national rights or prestige, must be considered the original cause of the trouble in Shanghai which culminated in the Mixed Court fracas of December 18th last and which was precipitated by the hasty action of the Consular Body under the influence of the Municipal Council.[30]

When the British demanded an indemnity of $80,000 (silver) for the losses sustained by British subjects, Rockhill wrote to Secretary Root: "I still fail to see the validity of the British claim, for how the Chinese Government can be held responsible for the maintenance of order in a settlement in which it has no right to have police, let alone an armed force, is not at all clear to my mind." [31]

---

[26] Rockhill to Root, November 6, 1905, Department of State Archives.

[27] Julius G. Lay to Rockhill, December 7, 1905, Rockhill Papers.

[28] *The Outlook,* December 30, 1905, p. 1052.

[29] Rockhill to Root, January 8, 1906, Department of State Archives.

[30] *Ibid.,* April 9, 1906.

[31] *Ibid.,* April 14, 1906.

The outbreaks at Lienchou and at Shanghai made clear that there were Chinese who disliked foreigners—but both outbreaks could be traced to local causes. Rockhill did not see in them, or in any of the other less serious disturbances, signs of a general movement of violence. Washington officials were still worried about the situation however, and, on February 26, President Roosevelt sent a strong note and a set of demands to be met by the government of China. The message, which by implication was a rejection of Rockhill's policy, was cabled to Rockhill by Secretary Root. It stated that events in China foreshadowed another outbreak of violence against foreigners. Evidence from many independent sources was showing that feelings of antagonism toward American citizens and interests in China were spreading without effective check by the government, "indeed the indications are that the apathy, if not the direct encouragement of the Imperial Government is behind the indifferent or unfriendly course of the provincial and local authorities." Officials failed to prevent injuries to the life and property of Americans and failed to punish those guilty of the crimes. The note also complained that there were unlawful combinations in restraint of trade. Because of these conditions the United States

> feels that it has perfect right to demand, first, that efficient measures be taken to prevent a renewal of the outrages of nineteen hundred; secondly, that all sympathizers with the anti-foreign movement, whether in high or low places, be sternly dealt with; thirdly, that ample indemnity be given for the murder or injury of American citizens to all sufferers who claim it, and that the provincial and municipal officers who have failed in their duty to protect them be punished; fourthly, that effective steps be taken to suppress inflammatory combinations in restraint of lawful trade and that the responsible delegates of sovereign power be punished for derelection in executing the proclaimed imperial will.[32]

Rockhill replied to Secretary Root that the disquieting reports from the United States about China were not justified. He denied that there was a widespread anti-American movement and he attributed the few recent disturbances to local causes. Moreover, he was optimistic about the future because of the desire among all classes of Chinese for independence from foreign control and exploitation. This goal could be achieved only if there was peace.[33]

While Rockhill did not believe there was danger of another outbreak of violence against foreigners, he delivered the President's message and pressed his demands. The view of Prince Ch'ing, head of the Foreign Office, was that while there were many disturbing rumors afloat and while revolutionists and "students of shallow learning" sought to weaken the government by creating an anti-foreign feeling among the Chinese, the masses of the people were loyal. He agreed to meet each of the President's demands to the best of his ability.[34] On March 6, an imperial edict was issued condemning the circulation of false reports

[32] Root to Rockhill, February 26, 1906, Department of State Archives.

[33] Rockhill to Root, February 26, 1906, Department of State Archives.

[34] *Ibid.*, March 5, 1906.

of an antiforeign movement and calling on students to cultivate loyalty to the state and cease interfering with foreign relations by putting forth wild proposals. Prince Ch'ing also called on local officials to give full protection to foreigners and their property.[35]

The United States was not content to rest having succeeded in getting the head of the Foreign Office to agree to meet its demands. Rockhill reminded the Foreign Office on March 17 that this must be followed by action, and he expressed the dissatisfaction of his government with the Liangkwang Viceroy who had failed to cooperate.[36] Rockhill had expressed the opinion, in the preceding September, that the central government would have to proceed with caution in southern China for fear of revolution. However, in March, after the Viceroy had caused considerable difficulty, Rockhill warned the Foreign Office that "if the Imperial Government was not willing or able to enforce its commands, the Powers would be driven to seek redress for injuries received or for protecting their people and their interests in their treaty rights, from the provincial authorities themselves." He also stated that while he was not instructed to make any specific demand for the punishment of officials who had failed to carry out their duties, he had been told "to express the great dissatisfaction of my Government with the general course pursued by the Viceroy of Canton. . . ." It was the last of a series of attempts to get the Imperial government to take a firm stand.

On April 21 Rockhill wrote to his old friend, Alfred E. Hippisley:

> It is very interesting at present to try and trace out who—or what group of persons, can be responsible for the systematic campaign of misrepresentations concerning everything in China, which is now going on. I think it is traceable to the native press and to irresponsible Japanese and perhaps Russians. Nobody else could gain anything by it. In Shanghai the foreign home-rulers—headed by J. O. P. Bland are responsible for much but not all. The business world in Shanghai has helped misrepresent things—especially some of those engaged in the American trade—for speculative purposes but Rodger's report on last year's trade shows that we have not suffered. I think that the Washington government is rapidly getting over its excitement.[37]

China's boycott was as successful as the Chinese could—with reason—have hoped it would be. Probably nothing short of military defeat would have caused the United States to open its doors to the Chinese. But the boycott did focus attention on the abuses Chinese had been subjected to, and, to a great degree, those abuses were removed.

Rockhill had been in a difficult position in the summer of 1905. Roosevelt and American commercial interests were alarmed. Knowing China as he did, Rockhill realized that his own government must not give way to impatience. Given time the native merchants would discover that the boycott was involving them in financial losses and that movement would be broken. At the same time

[35] *Ibid.*, March 7, 1906.

[36] *Ibid.*, March 17, 1906.

[37] Rockhill to Hippisley, April 21, 1906, Rockhill Papers.

he spared no effort in pressing the Chinese government to put an end to the boycott and made it clear to the Chinese Foreign Office that failure to do so would be considered a violation of treaty obligations. His firmness with the Chinese and the constant pressure he exerted in seeking to prevent the United States from taking extreme measures were important factors in bringing about the restoration of traditionally amicable relations between the two countries.

CHAPTER EIGHT

Between Two Worlds

It was not surprising that the Legation staff found Rockhill suffering from what they called "mental gout." The troubles growing out of the boycott would have tried a less melancholy man than Rockhill; in the summer of 1905, there were difficulties enough had there been no Chinese immigration question.

Shortly after assuming his duties as Minister to China, Rockhill received a letter from Roosevelt stating that some missionary interests had accused Rockhill of lacking sympathy with their cause.[1] Roosevelt, sensitive to criticism from such a politically powerful group, cautioned Rockhill. The President thought the charges grew out of the supposed use of the Sabbath day for meetings settling the claims following the Boxer uprising.[2]

While Rockhill had no great sympathy with the missionaries, he was sufficiently circumspect to recognize that no representative of the government of the United States could afford to appear indifferent toward the extension of Christianity. Replying to the President, Rockhill explained that, while he had nothing to do with the settlement of claims after the outbreak of 1900, there was "just a bit of truth however, in the Sunday story." Amused but irritated, he told Roosevelt: "My wife, horresco referens, used to receive visits Sunday afternoon, an old Washington fashion I like to keep up, and so many good missionaries did not come to see her, and I suppose were horrified. They might have submitted claims had they come, but they didn't." [3] He assured Roosevelt that the missionaries he had seen both in Shanghai and Peking had expressed pleasure in seeing him again in China and that he had, in turn, "assured them that their rights and interests, their work and their aspirations, were as dear to me as those of any other Americans and that I would do all in my power to uphold them." [4] No more was heard from the missionaries, and Rockhill dutifully defended them and presented their claims on occasions when they were victims of violence, although he showed no religious zeal for the redemption of the heathen.

Minor criticism came from another direction. In September, 1905, Edward H. Harriman, chairman of the Union Pacific Railway and the Pacific Mail Steamship Company, arrived in Peking after a visit to Japan where he had been launching a project for the purchase of the South Manchurian and the Trans-Siberian rail-

[1] President Theodore Roosevelt to W. W. Rockhill, May 18, 1905, Rockhill Papers.

[2] Rockhill to Roosevelt, July 7, 1905, Rockhill Papers.

[3] *Ibid.*

[4] *Ibid.*

roads. Rockhill shared as little of Harriman's zeal for the expansion of American investments in the Orient as he did of the Christian missionaries' enthusiasm for the salvation of souls. However, in accordance with previous letters of instruction from the State Department, he offered Harriman his assistance in getting commercial information, but the railroad magnate said that he had no business to transact in Peking. Still, Harriman left Peking with hostile feelings toward the Minister and parted with the threat of "taking the matter up" in Washington.[5]

Actually, it was not railroad investments but the question of a Court audience which caused the difficulty. After the Rockhill-Harriman interview, Harriman's secretary had come to say that his employer "desired to have the Imperial Palace opened to him so that he could visit it." Rockhill apparently manifested no enthusiasm for seeking his admission, and told the secretary that there was no possibility of the Manchu Court granting such a request if it were made. Because of the persistency of Harriman's representative, and against his own wishes, Rockhill made oral inquiries and found that there was no inclination to open the doors of the Imperial Palace to Harriman. Rockhill wrote to Prince Ch'ing and received a prompt and sharp refusal. Hoping to forestall criticism, Rockhill notified Secretary of State Elihu Root of the incident: "I was and still am of the opinion that it would be most impolitic to ask for extraordinary favors of the Chinese Government for traveling Americans. It would expose this Legation to many rebuffs from the Chinese, and angry comments, as in the present case, from disappointed countrymen." [6] Rockhill heard no more of the matter.

Overshadowing the difficulties with the missionaries and Harriman was the hubbub created by the cancellation of the Canton-Hankow railway contract, which was, up to that time at least, the most important concession acquired by Americans in China.[7] The right to build this strategic line had been acquired early in 1898 when China, faced with European demands for railway rights, had mildly welcomed the project as a means of counterbalancing the influence of the European powers.[8] The line was to cover a distance of about nine hundred miles. By the summer of 1905, the "rights recovery" movement, stimulated by Japan's victory over Russia, was under way, and the Chinese were determined to eliminate foreign control of railways and other business enterprises, including the concession of the American China Development Company to construct the Canton-Hankow line.[9]

---

[5] Rockhill to Secretary of State Elihu Root, November 28, 1905, Rockhill Papers.

[6] *Ibid.*

[7] William Barclay Parsons, *An American Engineer in China* (New York: McClure, Phillips & Co., 1900), p. 45.

[8] Thomas F. Millard, *The New Far East: An Examination into the New Position of Japan and Her Influence upon the Solution of the Far Eastern Question* (New York: Charles Scribner's Sons, 1906), p. 224.

[9] The Chinese opposed railroad construction because it was so frequently a means by which foreigners gained important political rights and also because there was much

The record of the American China Development Company reflected unfavorably upon the integrity and regard for commitments of American business. Soon after obtaining the concession, the company sold a majority of the stock to a syndicate of French and Belgian capitalists who were allegedly acting for the Russo-Chinese Bank. Rockhill learned the facts from the Secretary of the American Asiatic Association who deplored the sale.[10] Late in 1904 the stock changed hands again; this time a group of New York capitalists acquired control. Elihu Root, who was to succeed Secretary of State Hay the following year, represented the company in the negotiations.[11] These transactions in the ownership of stock were not accompanied by any significant progress on construction, and, in 1905, after an expenditure of three million dollars, only twenty-seven miles of track had been completed. In that year, China, dissatisfied because of the lack of any real progress on construction as well as the failure of the original stockholders to retain control, asserted her right under the original agreement to inspect the work and the accounts of the company.[12]

Before leaving Washington in April, 1905, Rockhill had sought to adjust the differences between the company and the Chinese Minister. His predecessor in Peking had also shown concern and had advised that a representative be sent to the provinces concerned to assure the people that this was a new company and controlled by Americans.[13] Nothing had been done. On the day following his arrival in Peking, Rockhill cabled the Secretary of State that sale of the concession would "gravely and permanently injure our interests here." He urged that the contract be amended to meet Chinese objections.[14]

A few days later he wrote a letter criticizing the company for making a muddle of its enterprise and advised that if it should now sell at an enormous profit Americans would suffer for years to come. Aside from the harmful effect on American commercial interests, the projected line would probably fall into the hands of Europeans and thereby become dangerous to American political interests.[15] In July, in response to a cable from President Roosevelt, Rockhill again severely criticized the company. He stated:

> Price fixed by the development company six millions three-quarters, a sum vastly in excess of outlay of company to date, plus liberal interest, is looked upon by

antipathy toward railroads on the part of the superstitious populace. Destruction of graveyards incidental to construction, and the cutting away of small hills supposed to be the residing place of beneficent spirits, led to popular opposition. Disturbance of these portended evil, and it was widely held that a railroad worked harm by permitting the good influences to drift away. Kenneth Scott Latourette, *The Chinese: Their History and Culture* (New York: Macmillan Co., 1943), II, 168.

[10] John Foord to Rockhill, June 24, 1904, Rockhill Papers.

[11] Rockhill to Secretary of State John Hay, June 7, 1905, Department of State Archives.

[12] Millard, *op. cit.*, p. 229.

[13] Rockhill to Hay, June 7, 1905, Department of State Archives.

[14] *Ibid.*, June 2, 1905.

[15] *Ibid.*, June 7, 1905.

all as excessively sharp practice of the shareholders. It is a blow to all our interests in China. It places our Government, which helped to secure the concession, in a false position. It serves to intensify anti-American feeling and aids our competitors in these markets. It has shaken belief in our business integrity, if consummated Americans will get no new concessions for years to come. . . .[16]

Rockhill received a sharp reply from the President, stating that he had shown the cable to Morgan and Ingraham, the interested American capitalists. The President was "astounded at the discrepancy between the facts as set forth therein [Rockhill's cable] evidently from information from Chinese Government and the facts as they actually are." Either the Chinese government or the Chinese Legation at Washington, wired Roosevelt, was "guilty of gross prevarication of truth." [17]

Unknown to Rockhill, shortly after he left for China, the Peking government, through its Minister in Washington, had threatened to annul the contract. The American China Development Company had then entered into a provisional settlement with the Chinese Minister to sell the railroad to the Chinese government for $6,750,000.[18] The company made no effort to have the Department of State intervene in its behalf; it was apparently content to sell at the price to which China had agreed.

Roosevelt was opposed to the sale but thought the company had no choice. Adee wired Rockhill: "The President does not see how we can submit to such a blow, especially as the concession was largely obtained through the action of the government as stated in your telegram. . . ." [19]

Rockhill, with no information from either the Chinese Board of Foreign Affairs or the Department of State, knew nothing of the Chinese Minister's action until he received the cable from Roosevelt on August 9. Therefore, he had centered his criticism on the company. This led Roosevelt to accuse him of a misapprehension of the facts.

Rockhill wrote a vigorous reply to the President's accusation. He offered evidence to the effect that the company was taking advantage of the Chinese desire to regain control of the railway by selling at an exorbitant price. He quoted Mr. Barclay Parsons, an official of the company, as saying that the sum of $6,750,000 had been fixed "to gauge the opposition of the Chinese to their Company," and the same official had termed the price large and practically prohibitive. In referring to the transaction, Chinese railway officials had laughed at what they called the "cleverness of the Americans." In view of these facts, Rockhill believed that he was justified in his criticism of the company. Concerning Roosevelt's accusation that he had "misapprehended" the facts, Rockhill reminded the State Department that while the negotiations had been going on in

[16] Rockhill to Root, July 26, 1905, Department of State Archives.

[17] Roosevelt to Rockhill, August 8, 1905, Department of State Archives.

[18] Rockhill to Root, August 14, 1905, Department of State Archives.

[19] Alvey A. Adee to Rockhill, August 15, 1905, Department of State Archives.

Washington, presumably not without its knowledge, not a word of information had been forwarded to him.[20]

The question arises as to whether the State Department knew of the negotiations between the company and the Chinese Minister. Elihu Root had represented the company in the negotiations prior to his becoming Secretary of State in June, and it seems improbable that Root was wholly uninformed of the transactions which were so important from the government's point of view.

With the facts furnished by Roosevelt, Rockhill pursued the subject at China's Foreign Office. There he met with evasion and what appeared to him as deliberate falsehood. Na-T'ung, Minister of Foreign Affairs, denied all knowledge of the reported annulment of the concession. With deep suspicions that the Peking government was guilty of misrepresentation, Rockhill cross-examined the Minister in the manner of a prosecuting attorney. He gave the following report of the conversation:

Rockhill: I would like to know if the contract for the Canton Hankow Railway has been annulled by the Chinese Government?

Na-T'ung: Not that I know of.

Rockhill: Has such an Edict been issued?

Na-T'ung: I have seen no such Edict, it has not been issued thro' my Board.

Rockhill: If that is the case, I suppose I may reply to the President that the recital of facts as set forth in the memorandum I have just handed you is not true, that the concession has not been cancelled and annulled, and that H. E. Liang has exceeded his authority in making such a memorandum of settlement with the American Company.

Na-T'ung: Oh no! I only said that I *had seen* no Edict to that effect, it may be that such Edict has been issued and went through the Grand Council. I will inquire of the Grand Council about it.

Rockhill: For the purpose of international relations the Foreign Office represents the Chinese Government, if therefore your office knows nothing of the facts I must conclude that the concession in question could not have been cancelled without Imperial Edict. Such Edict would I assume have to be communicated to you.

Na-T'ung: I will inquire of the Grand Council about it and let you know as soon as possible. I will also telegraph to Chang Chih-t'ung urging him to answer our previous telegram, at the same time I will wire H. E. Liang asking him upon what authority he based his statements.

Rockhill: Very well, if your Excellency can give me no more definite information; but I regret very much that you cannot give me more satisfactory information, and it will be particularly difficult for me to satisfactorily explain to my Government how the matter can be conducted by your diplomatic representative in America without your knowledge or approval. I may add that in view of Mr. Conger's note in January of this year . . . explaining my Government's position as regards the Hankow-Canton Railway concession, I do not believe that an annulment or cancellation of the concession without my Government having been informed of the fact can be recognized as valid by it.[21]

---

[20] Rockhill to Root, August 17, 1905, Department of State Archives.

[21] *Ibid.,* August 14, 1905.

This inquisition bore results. On the following day Rockhill received a letter from the Foreign Office which told the story of how China had sought to evade protests from the United States by handling the question through offices other than the Board of Foreign Affairs. The Grand Council had sent three confidential letters of instructions from the Emperor to Viceroy Chang Chih-tung directing him to find a way to cancel the concession. The Viceroy, thereupon, had advised the Emperor that the Chinese Minister in Washington be authorized to act jointly with him in gaining control of the projected railroad. A memorial was issued, and the Minister in Washington had acted according to instructions.[22]

The tactics employed by the government led Rockhill to charge the Chinese Foreign Office with falsehood and to deny the validity of the annulment. The Foreign Office had denied all knowledge of the edict, and yet both the President and Associate President of that office were members of the Grand Council which had received the memorial from Viceroy Chang Chih-tung requesting authority to regain control of the railroad. Rockhill held that the Board of Foreign Affairs was the Chinese government, insofar as the management of its international affairs was concerned, and therefore the United States could not "recognize as valid the action in such matters of any person or persons outside of the Foreign Office except as its agents and subject to its approval." [23]

In August the company completed final arrangements for the sale of the railroad concession, and the United States made no further effort to prevent annulment of the contract.[24] In a speech before the American Asiatic Association in 1914, Rockhill referred to the loss of the concession as the hardest blow the United States had suffered in China.[25] The sale of the controlling stock to European interests which China had feared, the failure to make any significant progress on construction, and the final sale at an extremely high price injured the reputation of American business. On the other hand, China's revoking of the concession created an extremely unfavorable impression on Roosevelt, although Rockhill did his best to put China's action in as favorable a light as possible.[26]

At the time that the American China Development Company was selling its concession for the Canton-Hankow railroad, Rockhill was apprehensive about

---

[22] *Ibid.*

[23] Rockhill to Root, August 22, 1905, Department of State Archives.

[24] Root to Rockhill, August 29, 1905, Department of State Archives.

[25] Speech before Asiatic Institute, New York, November 12, 1914, Rockhill Papers.

[26] Rockhill wrote: "In connection with the apparently devious ways in which the Chinese Government is dealing with the question of the cancellation of the American Company's concession, I am clearly of the opinion that it is in no way prompted by a desire to show hostility to America, but that it is a result of the strong opposition developed in the last two years against the Company in the Provinces of Hunan and Hupeh, and which the Imperial Government is fearful to oppose, as it might result in showing once again its weakness and inability to effectively cope with a strong opposition." Rockhill to Root, August 17, 1905, Department of State Archives.

the increased activities of the Germans in Shantung. Prior to the writing of the Open Door notes, and again during the Boxer negotiations, Germany had aroused Rockhill's suspicions. While in Shanghai, and again in Chefoo and Peking, in the spring of 1905, Rockhill was told that Germany was threatening to take over complete control of Shantung. The Consul-General at Chefoo furnished Rockhill with a long report covering German activities and, among other charges, held that the Germans were seeking exclusive mining privileges.[27]

Rockhill had been in Peking less than a week when he sent a message to the Department of State urging that a consular agency be established at Tsinan for the purpose of keeping a closer watch on the Germans. He warned that the German Legation was trying to gain control of the entire province, and reminded the Secretary of State that the German Minister had attempted earlier in the year to have the nominations for Governor of Shangtung submitted for his approval. Now there was further evidence that the Germans were pursuing aims inconsistent with their frequent assurances of respect for the Open Door and Chinese integrity. The British, Japanese, and Chinese were already alarmed by this threat, and Rockhill advised that it was so important for the United States to show an active interest "that, in the impossibility, without Congressional action, of creating a Consulate at Chi-nan-Fu, I deemed it advisable to request the Department to establish at least a Consular agency there." German aggressiveness was "so evident and so strong" that Rockhill further suggested

> whenever a favorable opportunity offers the Department should call the attention of the German Ambassador thereto and while expressing its disinclination to believe the reports concerning it, declare in the most emphatic way that such actions, if ever taken, would be most strongly resented by our Government as it would conflict with all German assurances. While we recognize the preferential rights acquired by Germany *in the territory* leased by her from China under the convention of March 6, 1898, we do not recognize that such rights extend beyond the leased area and in this contention we are supported by the oft repeated assurances of Germany itself.[28]

German policy assumed a less aggressive character soon after and, when questioned a year later on the subject, Rockhill reported that a change had taken place in the summer of 1905. Not only had Germany shown a friendlier attitude in her relations with the government of China, she had consented to participation in the commerce and industry of Shantung by other countries. He referred to the withdrawal of German troops from Shantung and to Germany's willingness to permit the British to share in railroad construction. While American Consul Fowler, stationed in Shantung, had expressed the view that American interests might be greatly developed if China did not fear German opposition, Rockhill wrote that it would not

> effect [*sic*] our interests a tittle; we would be no more enterprising in Shantung than we are in other provinces in which we have absolutely nothing to fear from

[27] Rockhill to Hay, June 7, 1905, Department of State Archives.

[28] *Ibid.*

any foreign or native opposition. American trade out here is distinctly lacking in enterprise. American capital can be too well employed at home to seek an outlet in China, where it may earn 4½ to 5 per cent, often with very considerable risk; and American products can be so well sold, in sufficient and ever-increasing quantities, by our present methods, that our merchants do not appreciate the necessity for adopting a more aggressive policy for securing a larger share of the trade in this country.[29]

Rockhill saw no reason to question German intentions, but some Americans were of a different opinion. When bids were turned in for the Whangpo Conservancy project, the largest engineering undertaking in China up to that time, the German bid was 50 per cent less than the highest. It was based upon the investigations made by an engineer attached to the staff of the German Consulate-General in Shanghai, a fact which the American Consul-General thought was an indication of "the way the wind is blowing in regard to German commercial processes and endeavors in China." [30]

In Washington the attitude toward Germany was also friendly. William Phillips, who had been a Legation secretary on Rockhill's staff in Peking, wrote to Rockhill:

> The Manchurian situation has changed a bit of late for Germany has *very confidentially* shaken hands with us and is in complete accord with our views. We have approached Great Britain and are endeavoring to get her to place a Consul in Harbin. Russia on her part has been very active in trying to enlist the sympathies of Europe to her side, with, we are told, a certain amount of success. However, if the United States, Great Britain and Germany can stand together out there we shall be able to assume a bold front.[31]

The cooperation of the United States and Germany, to which Phillips referred, was in the process of being realized in the fall of 1908. The United States was gratified by the cooperative attitude of Germany. The Kaiser, now anxious to postpone the possible breakup of China because of his own inability to benefit fully from such a development, hoped to bring about an alliance between his government and that of the United States in an attempt to preserve the status quo.[32]

Yuan Shih-k'ai, Grand Councilor and Senior Guardian of the Heir Apparent, was appointed to the Foreign Office in October, 1907. He took the initiative in seeking to arrange the proposed alliance with the United States and Germany.[33] An opportunity to sound out the State Department presented itself in November, 1908, when Tang Shao-yi, protégé of Yuan, went to Washington to express gratification for the return of the indemnity. Tang was instructed to seek Ameri-

[29] *Ibid.*, December 29, 1906.

[30] James L. Rodgers to Acting Secretary of State Robert Bacon, March 25, 1907, Department of State Archives.

[31] William Phillips to Rockhill, June 3, 1908, Rockhill Papers.

[32] John Gilbert Reid, *The Manchu Abdication and the Powers, 1908-1912: An Episode in Pre-War Diplomacy* (Berkeley: University of California Press, 1935), pp. 10, 22.

[33] *Ibid.*, p. 13.

can financial support for a more vigorous assertion of Chinese sovereignty in Manchuria, and then he was to go to Berlin to promote the contemplated alliance.[34] On the success of Tang depended not only China's ability to counteract the aggressiveness of Japan in Manchuria but also the official career of Yuan Shih-k'ai. Yuan's position was extremely shaky after the death of the Empress Dowager and the coming to power of the Prince Regent, an avowed enemy.

Neither China nor Yuan Shih-k'ai were saved by Tang's mission, for on the day that he arrived in Washington, the Root-Takahira Agreement was signed. The United States and Japan had agreed to support the status quo in the Pacific area, which presumably included Japan's special position in Manchuria and Yuan's attempt to enlist American support for the ousting of the Japanese from northern China collapsed. Japan promptly reminded the Regent of Yuan's failure and, early in January, 1909, Yuan was dismissed.[35]

Rockhill failed to see that Japan had won a victory at China's expense.[36]

---

[34] Tang Shao-yi, Governor of Fengtien, accepted Willard Straight's proposal to counteract Japanese influence in Manchuria by investment of American capital. Tang went to Peking in the spring of 1908 to promote the plan. Regarding Tang's mission to Peking, Croly writes: "His influence was considerable, for he was an important member of the party of Yuan-shi-Kai, then head of the Foreign Office and the dominant force in the government. He soon obtained the endorsement by the Empress Dowager of his plan. He also prepared for a journey to the United States in order to return thanks for the generosity of this country in remitting its share of the Boxer indemnity. The government after proposing first to send another emissary finally decided to commission Tang for this office and to conceal the real financial object of his visit behind the screen of this complimentary mission." Herbert Croly, *Willard Straight* (New York: Macmillan Co., 1924), p. 255.

On the basis of his study of the correspondence of the German Minister in Peking, Count von Rex, published in *Die Grosse Politik,* John Gilbert Reid concludes that Tang was scheduled to visit Germany where he was to promote an understanding between Germany, the United States, and China. Reid, *op. cit.,* p. 11, 16.

[35] Reid, *op. cit.,* p. 20.

[36] The Root-Takahira Agreement stated that the policy of both governments was directed "to the maintenance of the existing status quo" in the region of the Pacific Ocean. Each agreed to "respect the territorial possessions belonging to each other in said region." The signatories also promised to support "by all pacific means at their disposal the independence and integrity of China and the principle of equal opportunity for commerce and industry of all nations in that Empire." *Foreign Relations: 1908,* pp. 510-11.

This agreement has been subject to various interpretations by students of Far Eastern affairs. Thomas F. Millard takes the position that the United States was reasserting its historic policy of the Open Door and that Japan was forced to reach a settlement on outstanding issues in order to quiet war-talk, restore her credit abroad, check China's efforts to come to a closer understanding with the United States, and to allay suspicion of her Asiatic policy. Thomas F. Millard, *America and the Far Eastern Question* (New York: Moffat, Yard & Co., 1909), pp. 367-73.

Payson Treat states that Japan negotiated the agreement in order to reply to the unwarranted charges that she was violating the Open Door in Manchuria while "the American administration, in exchanging notes, testified to its belief in the good faith of Japan."

Instructed by the Department of State to inform the Chinese Foreign Office of the Root-Takahira Agreement, he was surprised when the first reaction in Peking was unfavorable. He discussed the terms of the agreement with the Chinese officials again, and reported that, after further explanation, there was no objection.[37]

Secretary of State Root, who, probably unwittingly, contributed to Yuan's fall, disapproved of the Regent's action, and on January 10, he authorized Rockhill to make joint representations with the British Minister as regards the dismissal of Yuan.[38] When Rockhill and Sir John Jordan, the British Minister, called on Prince Ch'ing on January 15, they were received in a friendly manner, and Rockhill gained the impression that Prince Ch'ing was glad they had taken this action. Prince Ch'ing thought Yuan Shih-k'ai might return to public life, as he was still young, but remarked that it was inexpedient for him to state the reason for the step taken by the Regent.[39] Three days later, Liang T'un-yen, Vice-President of the Foreign Office, met Rockhill, and told him the representations were excellent.[40] On January 20, Rockhill made the following note in his diary: "Root telegraphed 'highly commend your course (in matter of representations) in name of Dept. and of the President.' This is the first time I have received such a telegram." [41] That Root should have felt so strongly about supporting Yuan, the strongest opponent of Japanese expansion, seems to indicate that in entering into the agreement with Takahira, he had unknowingly appeased Japan.

Since the boycott of 1905 and the clash over the cancellation of the Canton-Hankow railroad concession, relations between China and the United States had been less cordial. The rift had also undermined the strong position which Rockhill had enjoyed with President Roosevelt. At the time of the boycott the German Ambassador to the United States reported that the President and Secretary of State were highly dissatisfied with Rockhill. According to Ambassador von Sternburg, they thought Rockhill had been in the Far East so long that he had come to look at questions from a Chinese, rather than an American, point of view.[42]

Payson J. Treat, *The Far East: A Political and Diplomatic History* (New York: Harper and Bros., 1928), pp. 402-03.

A number of other writers have viewed the notes as a recognition of Japan's special position in Manchuria. A. Whitney Griswold offers evidence that Roosevelt intentionally "qualified his allegiance to these doctrines" (the Open Door and China's territorial and administrative integrity). A. Whitney Griswold, *The Far Eastern Policy of the United States* (New York: Harcourt, Brace & Co., 1938), p. 131.

[37] Reid, *op. cit.*, p. 20.

[38] Rockhill's diary, Vol. II, entry January 10, 1909, Rockhill Papers.

[39] *Ibid.*, January 12, 1909.

[40] *Ibid.*, January 15, 1909.

[41] *Ibid.*, January 20, 1909.

[42] Speck von Sternburg to the German Foreign Office, cited by Alfred Vagts, *Deutschland und die Vereinigten Staaten in der Weltpolitik* (New York: Macmillan Co., 1935), II, 1250.

While Rockhill saw no reason to be disturbed by conditions in China, Roosevelt and Root were alarmed and impatient. The President ordered more troops to the Philippines in the spring of 1906. Charles Denby, adviser on Far Eastern affairs, and Robert Bacon, Assistant Secretary of State, were also uneasy about conditions in China. Denby expressed the view that it had been a serious error to encourage the withdrawal of German troops since they offered the best protection against an antiforeign outbreak. Bacon told von Sternburg that it was a serious mistake for Russia to withdraw from Manchuria inasmuch as her presence there had provided a necessary check on China.[43]

Although there was an unfriendly feeling in Washington toward China, Rockhill succeeded in gaining Roosevelt's support for the proposal that the Boxer indemnity be returned to China. The American portion of the indemnity was $25,000,000, to be paid by 1939 when the total paid by China would amount to approximately $50,000,000 including principal and interest. By 1905, all of the private claims, amounting to $2,000,000, had been paid. Hay and Rockhill were anxious to make rectifications, and Hay had confided to the Chinese Minister in Washington that a return of part of the indemnity was being considered. In December, 1904, Rockhill had drafted a message to Congress covering the question, and shortly after his arrival in Peking, he had suggested to Roosevelt that the indemnity be returned to China with the understanding that the fund be devoted to education. The proposal that the money be used for educating Chinese students in the United States originated with the Chinese. Rockhill considered this a more practical suggestion than that of Jeremiah Jenks, a prominent American in China, who had advocated that the indemnity be applied to the creation of a gold reserve fund.[44]

Roosevelt replied:

> I have all along been intending to make that recommendation very strongly in my message. I only hesitate on account of the action of the Chinese government, or its inaction, in the matter of the boycott and in the matter of this Hankow railway concession. I may do it anyhow, but I wish you would in the strongest way impress upon the Chinese Government that the chance of my getting any favorable action by Congress will be greatly interfered with by the failure of the Chinese to do justice themselves in such important matters as the boycott and the Hankow concession.[45]

Before action was taken, Consul Willard Straight urged that some of the funds be used for the economic development of Manchuria. According to Straight, William Howard Taft, then Secretary of War, was won over to his plan but it received no further support.[46] In 1908, action was taken along the line suggested by Rockhill. The United States retained $2,000,000 for possible future adjust-

[43] Vagts, *loc. cit.*

[44] Rockhill to Roosevelt, July 12, 1905, Rockhill Papers.

[45] Roosevelt to Rockhill, August 22, 1905, Rockhill Papers.

[46] Croly, *op. cit.,* p. 251.

ments and returned $10,785,286. From that date until 1924, when the remainder was waived, China's annual payments were credited to her to be used in the education of Chinese students in the United States.[47]

The money which the United States gave up was by no means a gift; it was no more than a return of the funds which China had paid in excess of the bill for damages. Rockhill viewed it as a simple act of justice to China. This did not detract from the good will promoted, for the code of ethics as practiced by nations did not require even this minimum act of justice. Whether the stipulation that the money be used for the education of Chinese in the United States proved wise is open to question. Contrary to a frequent assumption that the Chinese students, on their return to China, became agents of good will, they more often carried back deep resentment against the United States because they found themselves socially unacceptable on the American campus.

[47] Treat, *op. cit.*, p. 359.

CHAPTER NINE

Rockhill and the Japanese in Manchuria

Japan's re-adoption of an aggressive program in 1905 appears to have been an important first cloud portending the later storm which would break a generation later when the Japanese war machine overwhelmed southeastern Asia and the central Pacific. But to Rockhill at Peking the happenings in Manchuria were completely overshadowed by the Chinese boycott and the cancellation of the Canton-Hankow railway contract. Japan, rather than appearing as a potential enemy, was a trusted ally.

When Japan went to war against Russia in 1904, Rockhill—like President Roosevelt—considered that she was fighting America's battles. Rockhill's experience as adviser to the Department of State on Far Eastern affairs had left him with a deep distrust of Russia, the country which had consistently stood in the way of realization of American aims in China. Her boldness in acquiring leaseholds and railway rights in 1898, her ill-concealed desire to avoid making the commitments which Hay requested in 1899, her exploitation of the Boxer disturbances for the advancement of her interests in Manchuria, and the hostility which she manifested during the negotiation of the commercial treaty in 1903 were bound to antagonize an advocate of the Open Door and China's integrity. The Japanese challenge to Russian hegemony on the continent was, he felt, a blow at America's chief diplomatic antagonist, and Rockhill viewed the Japanese victory as a victory for the Open Door.

Theodore Roosevelt, while disturbed by the decisiveness of the Japanese victory, shared Rockhill's anti-Russian feelings. Before the peace negotiations had been completed at Portsmouth in the summer of 1905, he wrote to Rockhill: "bad as the Chinese are, no human being, black, yellow or white, could be quite as untruthful, as insincere, as arrogant—in short as untrustworthy in every way—as the Russians under their present system. I was pro-Japanese before, but after my experience with the peace commissioners I am far stronger pro-Japanese than ever." [1]

Rockhill was even more pro-Japanese than the President. When Roosevelt, somewhat uneasy about Japan's future policy, inquired of Rockhill as to the danger of the Chinese becoming mere followers of Japan, he replied that not only would the Chinese pursue an independent course but there was no reason to fear the recently victorious nation.

China has found out by its experience with Russia that it is unwise and even extremely dangerous for her to hand herself over to the tender mercies of any one

[1] President Theodore Roosevelt to W. W. Rockhill, August 29, 1905, Rockhill Papers.

> Power; she will never do it again, unless abandoned by all the other Powers, which is unlikely. China accepts Japanese guidance because she believes, and believes rightly I think, that the policy declared and followed by Japan in China must remain identical with that of the United States and Great Britain, to wit: the integrity of China and the "open door." Japan cannot depart from this policy without losing the support of not only our country and Great Britain but that of the business element of all nations which sees in it its only permanent safeguard.[2]

Rockhill's opinion that Japan would adhere to the Open Door and the concomitant policy of Chinese integrity, was based on his own experiences with Japanese diplomacy. Since 1895, when Russia, Germany, and France had forced her to relinquish the Liaotung Peninsula, Japan had pursued a policy almost identical with that of the United States. Her unreserved acceptance of the Hay formula in 1899, her complete cooperation at the time of the Boxer revolt, the strong support she gave to the views of the United States in the Boxer negotiations, and her advocacy of the Open Door in the years immediately preceding the outbreak of war in 1904 convinced Rockhill that Japan was a permanent diplomatic ally of the United States. But diplomacy is at best a rule-of-thumb game, and while all of the history of the last ten years supported Rockhill, the next storm was brewing in Japan.

Viewing Japan as a friendly power, Rockhill permitted himself to support his opinion with arguments which, however logical, bore little relationship to facts. In an address before the Naval War College at Newport, in August, 1904, he had said that in the struggle for the control of the potential wealth of China the land powers presented the real danger, since they would find it necessary to occupy strategic and economically important parts of the country. A weak, inefficient, and corrupt China would serve their purposes. In sharp contrast the nations which depended on sea power merely required access to the seaports and the Yangtze River in order to achieve economic control. They would benefit by the strengthening of China inasmuch as a strong central government would be able to comply with the demands of the foreigner.[3] Given these premises, Japan, as a naval power, might be relied upon to work with the United States and Great Britain.

Rockhill may have employed sound logic but the history of Japanese foreign policy, neither before nor after 1904, supported the generalizations he presented before the War College. To be sure Japan had pursued a waiting policy of temporary cooperation since 1894, but the history of Japanese expansionism went back to Hideyoshi in the sixteenth century. British conquest of vast territories also contradicted Rockhill's theory, and careful examination of the history of colonization would have indicated that sea powers were at least as likely to absorb backward areas as were land powers. Japan was to illustrate abundantly that Rockhill was mistaken.

---

[2] Rockhill to Roosevelt, July 7, 1905, Rockhill Papers.

[3] Lecture given by Rockhill at the United States Naval War College, August 5, 1904, Rockhill Papers.

At the very time that Rockhill was assuring Roosevelt that neither China nor the United States need fear Japan, the people of Tokyo were rioting and venting their spleen on the United States. They considered the United States responsible for their failure to get an indemnity and all of Saghalin. For days, troops bivouacked on the grounds of the American Embassy in order to protect it from angry mobs.[4]

In discounting the Japanese threat, Rockhill failed to give due weight to the fact that, by the Treaty of Portsmouth, Japan won a dominant position on the continent of Asia. The extensive Russian rights in southern Manchuria—which included two leaseholds, the area's most important railroad, and the many privileges which went with these—all infringed on China's sovereignty, and they were now Japan's. Japan was in a stronger position than Russia had been before the war. The new Far Eastern power had no problem of security in Europe to affect calculations concerning China. Russia had been weak on the sea; Japan had a powerful fleet, the home bases of which were close to the scene of any prospective operations. In addition, Japan was allied with Great Britain, the only nation which could challenge her in Pacific waters. Before the war, her relatively weak position dictated a conciliatory China policy; she was no longer weak after the negotiations at Portsmouth. This Rockhill failed to appreciate.

When it came to forming a correct estimate of China's strength, Rockhill was on safer ground. While Japan's victory over a Western power gave rise to the first stirring of nationalism among young Chinese, the Young China movement was richer in enthusiasm than in practical ideas for reform.[5] Although somewhat successful in their boycott of American goods, the Chinese nationalists gave little evidence of being prepared to carry through a constructive program, and, as for the group in power, the problems they confronted called for stronger leadership than they could offer. Rockhill, completely realistic concerning China's statesmen, wrote:

> The lack of any settled policy among the high officers of the Chinese Government, I refrain from using the word statesmen as I fear there is not one to be found in China at the present day, is terribly evident. Indecision and a determination to drift with any current is shown on every side. It is manifest to the most casual observer that China is quite unable to manage her international affairs without strong support and constant pressure from without.[6]

Rockhill and Roosevelt hoped to work with the Japanese in the strengthening of China and in the preservation of the Open Door. In July, 1905, Rockhill wrote Roosevelt:

---

[4] Lloyd C. Griscom, *Diplomatically Speaking* (New York: Literary Guild of America, Inc., 1940), p. 262.

[5] J. O. P. Bland, *Recent Events and Present Policies in China* (Philadelphia: J. B. Lippincott Co., 1912), pp. 24, 73.

[6] Rockhill to John Hay, July 1, 1905, Department of State Archives.

I do not think that the Japanese will endeavor to secure control of China, but will adhere strictly to their declared policy, which alone can make a lasting peace in this part of the world possible. That Japan will try to get as much of the markets of China and of Russia as she can supply I have no doubt, that she can and will help China to become a stronger, richer and more responsible Power is true, but that this will permanently disturb the balance of power in the East, seems to me highly improbable.[7]

While Rockhill was optimistic, the Chinese, apprehensive concerning the Japanese-Russian negotiations at Portsmouth, proposed sending a representative to stand guard over their interests. Rockhill, anxious to forestall this move, advised against it and assured the Manchu-Chinese officials that China's sovereign rights could not be impaired at the conference and any questions concerning them would presumably be discussed later.[8]

Peking's fears were not allayed, and the Wai Wu Pu sent a dispatch declaring that it would not recognize any arrangement transferring Russia's rights in the Liaotung Peninsula to Japan. To the Secretary of State, Rockhill confided: "It seems highly probable that Japan will insist on the reversion to her of the territory leased by China to Russia in 1896, situated in the Liaotung Peninsula, but, as I have repeatedly told the Chinese, it cannot be doubted that Japan will eventually make an agreement with China for the transfer of such rights." [9] Such prospects offered slight comfort to the Chinese.

In September, the Treaty of Portsmouth was completed, providing for Japan's taking over of the Russian rights in Port Arthur and Dalny exactly as the Chinese had feared. Roosevelt wired Rockhill: "In my judgment China cannot with propriety question efficacy of this transfer or hesitate to allow Japanese all the rights the Russians were exercising. If China shall contrive any trouble about the transfer in question you will at the proper time state this strongly to the Chinese Government. Please inform Japanese Minister of the contents of this telegram." [10]

Having given their approval to Japan's acquisition of the Russian rights in Manchuria in September, 1905, Roosevelt and Rockhill two months later poured their blessings on Japan's extinction of Korean independence. Baron Komura informed Rockhill that, while Japan did not request it, the withdrawal of the legations in Seoul would be appreciated. Rockhill cabled the Secretary of State, and the United States acted at once, the first nation to withdraw from Korea.[11] Rockhill received a note of appreciation from Baron Komura expressing the opinion that Rockhill's support had undoubtedly had great weight.[12] To Willard Straight, Secretary of Legation at Seoul, his country's action was shameful: he compared the withdrawal to rats deserting a sinking ship.

---

[7] Rockhill to Roosevelt, July 7, 1905, Rockhill Papers.

[8] Rockhill to Hay, July 1, 1905, Department of State Archives.

[9] Rockhill to Secretary of State Elihu Root, July 8, 1905, Department of State Archives.

[10] Roosevelt to Rockhill, September 11, 1905, Department of State Archives.

[11] Rockhill to Root, November 22, 1905, Department of State Archives.

[12] Baron Komura to Rockhill, November 26, 1905, Rockhill Papers.

In December, 1905, Japan concluded a treaty with China transferring to Japan the former Russian rights and giving that country additional privileges in a series of secret provisions. Baron Komura notified Rockhill of some of the provisions on the day the treaty was signed, including an agreement calling for the opening of sixteen localities in Manchuria to international trade and residence. Whether he was told about all of the others is not known, but his report to the Secretary of State makes it appear unlikely.[13] He made no comment on the treaty other than to say that the Chinese were extremely suspicious of Japanese motives and hedged on every point. Japan had gained a strong foothold in Manchuria without the United States voicing protest; apparently neither the President nor the United States Minister at Peking sensed a threat to American interests.

Japan embarked on a policy of granting privileges in Manchuria to her own nationals which violated the principle of equal commercial opportunity to which she had agreed. As early as June, 1905, Lloyd Griscom, United States Ambassador at Tokyo, cited two telegrams appearing in a Japanese newspaper stating that certain towns in Manchuria would be opened exclusively to Japanese traders.[14] Evidence accumulated during the next two years proved that Japan permitted goods of her own nationals to enter Manchuria free of duty, that Japanese goods were carried at lower rates on the Japanese-owned railroads than goods originating in other countries, that the Japanese military excluded foreign goods entirely from some areas. While Rockhill was slow to evince any concern in these violations of the Open Door, American commercial interests were not tardy in protesting. In April, 1906, Acting Secretary of State Robert Bacon brought a British-American tobacco company's complaint to Rockhill's attention.[15] In July, Swift and Company likewise complained that Japan was admitting its own goods free of duty in Manchuria. During the same month Rockhill received a report from the American Association of China making the same allegation.[16] Disturbed by a slump in trade, the Association had sent three merchants to Manchuria to investigate. These emissaries found that the Japanese imported their own merchandise into Manchuria by way of Dalny paying neither duty nor *likin*.[17]

These charges caused no alarm on the part of Rockhill who, as late as July, 1906, attributed the slump in trade to surpluses piled up during the war which later gutted the market.[18] He was not alone in this opinion; many others, including the American Consul at Shanghai, attributed the decline in trade to

[13] Rockhill to Root, December 22, 1905, Department of State Archives.

[14] Lloyd C. Griscom to Rockhill, July 15, 1905, Rockhill Papers.

[15] Acting Secretary of State Robert Bacon to Rockhill, April 20, 1906, Department of State Archives.

[16] *Ibid.*, July 31, 1906.

[17] John Gilbert Reid, American Association of China, to Rockhill, July 2, 1906, Department of State Archives.

[18] Rockhill to Reid, July 16, 1906, Department of State Archives.

the same cause.[19] The Japanese Minister admitted the irregularities in an interview with Rockhill late in July, 1906.[20] While Rockhill did not think the Japanese had brought about the shrinking of the market for American goods, he did not deny that the Japanese were enjoying special privileges. But he viewed it as a temporary situation due to the influence of the Japanese military rather than to any settled policy on the part of the Japanese government.

Rockhill's equanimity gave his reports to Washington a tone of intellectual aloofness. The solution to the problem of Japanese evasion of Chinese import duties was the establishment of customhouses throughout the area, and this Rockhill urged upon the Peking government. When the Manchu-Chinese continued to sit idly by, apparently unperturbed by the loss of revenue, Rockhill calmly explained the forces at work. Japan was slow to restore normal conditions and to complete evacuation of Manchuria, preferring to wait until Russia took steps to stabilize conditions in northern Manchuria where her troops were stationed. Russia delayed because she wished to see what concessions Japan would win from Peking, expecting to demand similar privileges for herself. Peking was dilatory because high officials hoped foreign commercial interests would criticize Japan, compelling her to evacuate; China had not met Japan's demands for special privileges in Manchuria hoping some change would make this unnecessary. China did not even approach Russia on the question of establishing customs on the northern frontier, believing that Russia would not yield on this question unless China confirmed mining rights and other concessions claimed by the Russians.[21] It was difficult to insist that the Chinese start a game in which all the cards were stacked against them.

Rockhill seemed to be content to wait. He thought the United States need not fear that Japan would exclude American capital from Manchuria, for she would need foreign capital to develop the area. Moreover, American business methods were partly responsible for the slump in trade. Americans relied on Chinese agents when direct relations with the customers would have been more effective.[22] Rockhill was also disgusted by American business men who, for some strange reason, seemed to assume that advertising in English would bring them Chinese customers.

The lack of aggressiveness on the part of American business did not alter the fact that Japan was taking unfair advantage of the situation. When the trade returns for 1906 were announced, Rockhill notified the State Department that the total value of Japanese products imported into Manchuria was £2,600,000 and of this amount only £300,000 passed through Newchwang where it was sub-

[19] James L. Rodgers to Rockhill, July 6, 1906, Department of State Archives.

[20] Rockhill to Root, July 31, 1906, Department of State Archives.

[21] *Ibid.*, August 15, 1906.

[22] *Ibid.*, October 11, 1906.

ject to import duties.[23] The continued Japanese violations a year after the close of military operations—when she could no longer reasonably plead military necessity—caused the State Department to take a sterner course. In a memorandum for the Secretary accompanying one of Rockhill's notes, Charles Denby advised: "I take the liberty to offer the opinion that in dealing with Japan on any matter whatever this Government should be influenced not by what she says but by what she does and that a far-reaching motive should be sought in every step of her diplomacy." [24] Others, too, were alarmed. Willard Straight, American Consul at Mukden, was extremely critical of the Japanese and won their enmity by his constant surveillance of their activities.[25] On Consul Straight's recommendation, Minister Rockhill sent a consular agent to Antung where the Japanese had bought up all available sites in the city and the immediate vicinity.[26] The American official received a cold reception.[27]

The long delay and recurring complaints of American merchants caused the Department of State to take energetic action in May, 1907. Instructions were sent to the ambassadors at St. Petersburg and Tokyo, directing them to impress on the respective foreign offices the interest of the United States in the restoration of normal conditions in Manchuria. A copy was sent to the American Embassy in London and it was suggested that it would be greatly appreciated should the British government see fit to address the same governments on the subject. The British replied that this had already been done.[28] On May 30,

[23] *Ibid.*, May 17, 1907.

[24] Charles Denby to Root, February 2, 1907; Memorandum attached to a dispatch from Rockhill to Root, December 28, 1906, Department of State Archives.

[25] Croly, *op. cit.*, p. 258.

[26] Willard Straight to Rockhill, May 2, 1907, Rockhill Papers.

[27] "Four days after my arrival at post I made my official call upon Mr. Okabe, the local Japanese Consul. A few moments after presenting my card to one of his secretaries, I was ushered into his office, and hardly had we finished the customary introductory salutations and seated ourselves before he addressed me, speaking in Japanese, with the abrupt inquiry: 'What's the meaning of this sudden opening of an American consulate at Antung? Might it be the result of Mr. Straight's recent visit here?'

"Changing the trend of the conversation, he then informed me that over two-thirds of the interests in this district were, as I was probably aware, Japanese and not Chinese, and suggested that, inasmuch as this was the case, I ought to have a Japanese secretary in my office, whom he would be willing to supply. I politely declined his offer and assured him that I myself possessed as extensive a knowledge of the Japanese language as I should have occasion to use. He then repeated his offer, stating that, while such was probably the case, he would be pleased to detail a student from his office who was anxious to learn English and that I would be put to no expense whatever for his services. I again declined, informing him that unfortunately not only was I prohibited from expending government funds for unnecessary services, but my regulations also forbade my employing any one in my office without remuneration." Charles J. Arnell to Straight, July 7, 1907, Department of State Archives.

[28] Root to the American Legation, Peking, May 22, 1907, Department of State Archives.

Rockhill telegraphed that Prince Ch'ing, President of the Board of Foreign Affairs, greatly appreciated the assistance "The United States were giving China now as before Russian-Japanese War since it strengthened greatly Governments hands." [29] In July, customhouses were opened at Dairen and Antung but there was delay in northern Manchuria, where customs were not collected until the end of August, 1907.[30]

The opening of customhouses did not solve the problem of the Open Door in Manchuria. Japan was pursuing a policy quite as inimical to American interests as Russia had done prior to the war. Rockhill received reports that Japanese officials were exempting their fellow nationals from taxation; that hundreds of Japanese were living and doing business in parts of Manchuria not yet open to trade; that the holding of property which had been seized by the military was being continued; that special railroad rates applied to Japanese goods.[31] The Minister was extremely cautious in making accusations against the Japanese, but he frequently forwarded the reports of Japanese violations to the State Department.

In 1907, as Japan continued to violate the principles of the Open Door, Rockhill lost some of his former confidence in the Japanese. In a letter to the Secretary of State on August 8, he referred to the assurance given the previous winter by the Japanese Minister in Peking regarding the seizure of land by the military authorities at Antung. He expressed regret that as yet nothing had been done by Japan "except in the way of extending and further fastening her hold on that important commercial and strategic locality." He also criticized the Japanese claim that railway-borne goods crossing the China-Korean frontier should be exempted from one-third duty.[32]

In Washington, the Roosevelt administration had likewise reached the conclusion that Japan had no intention of abiding by the Open Door in Manchuria. In 1909, the outgoing administration forwarded a memorandum to Philander C. Knox, the new Secretary of State, summarizing its Far Eastern policy. Concerning Manchuria, the memorandum said: "Treatment of American imports into Manchuria is being jealously watched by the foreign service in that part of the world, in order to make sure that the success of American exporters to the Orient shall depend upon their own efforts, unhampered by any discrimination on the part of foreign Governments." [33]

[29] Rockhill to Root, May 30, 1907, Department of State Archives.

[30] *Ibid.*, June 19 and August 25, 1907.

[31] Arnell to Rockhill, July 10 and 18, 1908, Department of State Archives.

[32] Rockhill to Root, August 8, 1908, Department of State Archives.

[33] Memorandum to Philander C. Knox from the Roosevelt administration, March [?], 1909, Correspondence of Philander C. Knox, Library of Congress.

CHAPTER TEN

Rockhill and the Dalai Lama of Tibet

An unusual honor came to Rockhill in 1905 when he was asked to serve as adviser to "The Sincerely Obedient, Reincarnation-helping, Most Excellent, Self-existent Buddha of the West," the Dalai Lama of Tibet. Having devoted long years of study to the ancient Buddhist scriptures and hazarded his life in exploration of Tibet, Rockhill was able to appreciate fully the Dalai Lama's exalted position of God-King. So holy is the Dalai Lama in the eyes of his people, that they are never permitted to look directly at him.

The choosing of a Dalai Lama is unique. Before he dies (he cannot marry) he tells those around him where he will reincarnate. Not until three or four years after his death is his successor—a child of three or four, of high or low birth—chosen in accordance with several physical signs which supposedly distinguish him from ordinary mortals—large ears, eyes and eyebrows that curve upwards, marks of tiger skin on legs, two pieces of flesh near the shoulder-blades indicating the other two hands of Shenrezig, and the imprint of a conch-shell on the palm of one hand. The person thus chosen becomes both temporal and spiritual leader of his people.

Tibet's theocratic government has long been determined to isolate itself economically, culturally, and politically from the rest of the world. When Rockhill explored Tibet, the country carried on no trade beyond its own borders and rigidly enforced a policy of excluding travelers, including missionaries, by threatening capital punishment for any official who tolerated them. Except for its recognition, since 1729, of Chinese sovereignty and the early penetration of Buddhism from India, Tibet had as little relationship with the outside world as America prior to the coming of the white man. While a tributary state of the Manchu dynasty, the only symbol of Chinese sovereignty at the capital at Lhasa was a small and impotent garrison of Chinese troops.

By 1900 the dreaded foreign intrusion could no longer be held at bay. Strategically located between British India on the south and not far from Russia on the north, Tibet was of great interest to both powers. In 1904 the British dispatched a military expedition under Sir William Younghusband. Rather than endure the disgrace of negotiating with the British, the Dalai Lama fled.

While the Dalai Lama was scampering off to Outer Mongolia in a manner quite out of keeping with divinity, Rockhill, then an adviser to the State Department, had written to Ambassador Joseph Choate in London instructing him to remind the Foreign Office that the severance of Tibet from China might serve as a precedent in other parts of the Manchu Empire, a development the

United States had long sought to forestall.[1] Great Britain accomplished her aims in a trade treaty without taking over Tibet and thereby nominal Chinese suzerainty was preserved.

The Dalai Lama soon learned that the removal of the British threat was accompanied by a new determination on the part of China to exercise closer control. When he fled Tibet, China deposed him, but his people continued to refer all matters to him for decision. Apprehensive of Chinese pressure should he return to Lhasa, the Dalai Lama remained at Urga in Mongolia.

While at Urga, he inquired of a Russian scientist about Western scholars who had studied the Tibetan language and who had an interest in the Yellow Church. The Russian referred him to Rockhill, and the Dalai Lama asked that Rockhill communicate with him.[2] A lengthy correspondence ensued and Rockhill met frequently with the Dalai Lama's agents in Peking.[3]

Wholly ignorant of the outside world and more particularly of the complications of international diplomacy, he looked to Rockhill for advice and hoped that the American Minister would intervene in his behalf at the Manchu Court which now threatened to limit Tibetan autonomy. The results were not entirely satisfactory to the Dalai Lama who wrote: "Through the medium of the [American] Minister we have several times reported to the golden ear of the Manchu Emperor. We have been writing for six or seven months, but we have not heard any of the illuminating commands [of the Manchu Emperor] in reply." [4] This letter to Rockhill was accompanied by gifts including a ceremonial scarf and a gilt copper image of the Buddha Amitagus.

Although Rockhill believed that Tibet was doomed to lose its former autonomy under Chinese rule and he could offer no solution to the Dalai Lama's problem, the correspondence continued. In June, 1908, Rockhill decided to visit the Dalai Lama who had now moved to the Lamasery of Wu-t'ai shan in the Chinese province of Shansi. He walked most of the way, going as far as twenty miles a day, an accomplishment which prompted him to write to William Phillips, "Not so bad for a man who hardly ever takes any exercise here, is it?"

Never prone to dramatize, Rockhill, for once, was ebullient, describing his meeting with the Dalai Lama as "the most unique experience I have ever had."

[1] Secretary of State John Hay to Joseph Choate, June 3, 1904, Department of State Archives. Rockhill's writing of almost all instructions concerning the Far East during this period and the presence of a draft bearing an earlier date in the Rockhill Papers suggest that he may have been responsible for the protest to London.

[2] Stcherbatski to W. W. Rockhill, August 17, 1905, Rockhill Papers in the possession of Miss Marion Crutch of Litchfield, Connecticut.

[3] Rockhill to President Theodore Roosevelt, June 30, 1908, Roosevelt Papers, Library of Congress.

[4] Dalai Lama to Rockhill, 1905, Rockhill Papers in the possession of Miss Crutch. The exact date of this letter is missing.

He found his host a vigorous young man, alert, intelligent, and friendly. The Dalai Lama was dressed in an imperial yellow satin gown and wore a bright vermilion silk shawl over his left shoulder and around his body. His boots were yellow with blue braiding. Sipping tea and partaking of sweetened rice, Rockhill and his host had a long conversation in Tibetan, giving most of their attention to the political situation. Rockhill was received again the next day, and on this occasion advised the Dalai Lama that Great Britain had no designs on his country and that Tibet should "establish close trade relations with India and cultivate friendly relations with neighboring states, but especially with India, his [the Dalai Lama's] closest neighbor." [5]

On his return to Peking, Rockhill wrote a twelve-page letter to President Roosevelt.

> There is much more I could say of this trip but I fear I have, in my gratifications over it, said too much already. I felt a deeper and more complete satisfaction with two interviews with the mysterious potentate and incarnation of the god Shenrezig than would any one who had not, like myself, given so many years of their life to Tibet. To be seated talking familiarly with the Tale Lama, with one of his abbots standing behind me, with His Holiness' fly-flapper keeping the flies off my head, and he seeing that my tea cup was filled with hot tea, asking me to open a correspondence with him, to be his councillor and friend; it was all too extraordinary. I could not believe my ears and eyes.[6]

Theodore Roosevelt fairly tingled with curiosity on receiving this account. The President replied in a tone of admiration:

> I think that is one of the most interesting and extraordinary experiences that any man of our generation has had. There has been nothing like it, so far as I know. Really, it is difficult to believe that it occurred! I congratulate you, and I congratulate the United States upon having the one diplomatic representative in the world to whom such an incident could happen.
>
> Now how shall I acknowledge the box containing the Buddha, and the big white silk Katag? What kind of a present should I send him in return? I have not the vaguest idea what the Tale Lama would like. I sent the Pope a copy of my books. It is just possible that he glanced at the outside of the cover of one; but I do not know that the Tale Lama would even care to do as much as this. Will you let me know? [7]

Before Rockhill had replied, Roosevelt wrote again explaining the use he had made of Rockhill's letter.

> Your letter containing the account of your extraordinary interview with the Tale Lama struck me as so important from the standpoint of the British Government that I let Bryce show it to certain of the highest officials. I enclose you a copy of his letter, from which you will see how much it impress them. If we can do a good turn to England in this matter I shall be glad; and if you find out anything as to

[5] Rockhill to Roosevelt, June 30, 1908, Roosevelt Papers.

[6] *Ibid.*

[7] Roosevelt to Rockhill, August 1, 1908, Rockhill Papers in the possession of Miss Crutch.

what passes between the Lama and the Chinese at Peking, pray let me know about it in full. . . .[8]

Rockhill's account of his interview made a favorable impression in London where Sir Edward Grey, Foreign Secretary, was happy to learn that the American Minister had assured the Dalai Lama that Great Britain had no designs upon Tibet and only wished to carry on trade relations.[9]

The God-King of Tibet now faced a government skilled in intrigue and deception. The Empress Dowager of China, anxious lest disorder in Tibet lead to foreign intervention, wished to seize control. It would be easier to introduce the changes among the disorderly lamas if the Dalai Lama returned to Lhasa, the Tibetan capital, and gave the Chinese reforms his divine blessing. The Dalai Lama, fearing the worst, refused to return. Provoked by his lingering in Shansi, the Manchu-Chinese officials invited him to Peking. His Holiness hesitated but finally concluded that a refusal would merely antagonize the Chinese without any gain to himself.[10]

Never was a political ruler deprived of his powers with more grandiose ceremony. High civil and military officials escorted the Dalai Lama from the Buddhist lamasery to the nearest railway terminal. In Peking, a troop of mounted infantry with drawn swords accompanied by four mounted buglers preceded the Dalai Lama in the long procession to the temple outside the city where he was to stay. Twenty men carried the great yellow chair in which His Holiness sat carefully curtained from view. In front of the temple stood rows of priests in long, yellow robes welcoming the supreme pontiff of their church.

The day after his arrival in Peking, the Dalai Lama sent one of his officers to Rockhill with the request that Rockhill come to see him. Rockhill presented himself to the Dalai Lama, accompanied by his entire Legation staff. He found His Holiness "in a much less happy frame of mind than when I had seen him last; he was evidently irritable, preoccupied and uncommunicative." Rockhill later concluded that the Dalai Lama had little interest in his own people and that he was merely intent on preserving his own privileges.[11]

On October 8, 1908, an imperial rescript announced the arrangements for the reception of the Dalai Lama by the Empress Dowager and the Emperor. While this was a great honor, it was so planned as to impress the guest with the lowness of his own position. He was carefully instructed as to his every move during the ceremony, the presents he was to give, and the words to be used in expressing gratitude for imperial favors. Most objectionable to the Dalai Lama

[8] *Ibid.*, September 7, 1908.

[9] Roosevelt enclosed a copy of the letter he had received from James Bryce. This is included in the Rockhill Papers in the possession of Miss Crutch.

[10] Rockhill to Roosevelt, November 8, 1908, Rockhill Papers in the possession of Miss Crutch.

[11] Rockhill to Roosevelt, November 8, 1908, Rockhill Papers in the possession of Miss Crutch.

was the requirement that he perform three kneelings and nine prostrations, a mark of obeisance which had not been required of the last Dalai to visit Peking—some two hundred years before.[12]

While these honors were being bestowed, the Dalai Lama was virtually a prisoner of the heavy guard placed at the temple where he resided. Aware of the plan to deprive him of his temporal powers, he sent Dorjieff, one of his abbots, to consult with Ivan Korostovetz, the Russian Minister. Dorjieff received no encouragement from Korostovetz who said that he had no advice to give and that Russia had given up the policy of advising and supporting Eastern rulers. He suggested that Dorjieff see Rockhill, the representative of an absolutely disinterested power.[13]

Rockhill as usual was cautious in his conversation with the Dalai Lama's representative. He told Dorjieff that the duties, rights, and prerogatives of the Dalai Lama and his predecessors had been subject to the decision of the Emperor of China ever since Tibet became a vassal state of the Manchu dynasty almost two hundred years earlier. Insofar as the Chinese press had reported the proposed reforms, he could not see what objection the Dalai Lama could have to them. Dorjieff replied that the Dalai Lama did not object to military reforms nor to the extension of education in Tibet but he wanted assurance that his church would be maintained in all its honors and that he would continue to have the right to submit directly to the throne any memorials (requests) he might wish. Rockhill expressed his own conviction that nothing would be done to lessen the dignity of the church in Tibet. Concerning the right to forward memorials directly to the throne, he stated that he believed the Dalai Lama was entirely justified in asking for it, but suggested that it would be wisest first to ascertain informally how such a request would be received.[14]

On November 3, the last of a series of imperial decrees concerning Tibetan affairs was issued. The Dalai Lama, hitherto enjoying the rank of "The Most Excellent, Self-existent Buddha of the West," was now elevated to "The Sincerely Obedient, Reincarnation-helping, Most Excellent, Self-existent Buddha of the West" and given an annual allowance of 10,000 *taels*. With these amenities taken care of, the imperial rescript went on to order the Dalai Lama's immediate return to Tibet, warned that he must be reverently submissive, and that anything he might have to report must be submitted to the Chinese Resident of Tibet.[15]

Having received these honors as well as orders encompassing the end of his temporal powers, the Dalai Lama was told by the Chinese officials that he must offer thanks in accordance with the form they had prepared. Although willing

---

[12] *Ibid.*

[13] *Ibid.*

[14] *Ibid.*

[15] A copy of a translation of the imperial edict is among the Rockhill Papers in the possession of Miss Crutch.

to express thanks for the honors he had received, the Dalai Lama was unwilling to thank the Chinese for depriving him of the right to send memorials to the throne directly. Instead he sought to include a request that this right be restored.[16]

But the Chinese were adamant in their demand that he sign the letter of thanks they had prepared, and the Dalai Lama once again sent his agents to see Rockhill. The Dalai Lama's cause was lost, and Rockhill told the agents so. In his notes on the conversation, Rockhill recorded:

> I went over the question carefully with the Khampo but saw no way out of it. The Chinese Gov't. has him at their mercy. I told him finally that the Dalai was the Emperor's subject, he could give or take away. . . . He had received many honors, the Chinese gov't. had settled to his satisfaction the difficulties with India, he must take the bitter with the sweet and I thought he should not delay long for it might be that the Empress expected a prompt reply undue delay would cause offense.
>
> . . . I said the Dalai must decide in his wisdom what to do, I could not, as much as I regretted it, advise him. I saw no way out of the *impasse* in which he was.
>
> He said he would report to the Dalai what I had said that they found I could do nothing but they were very grateful. They had no friend here but me.[17]

To Roosevelt he confided that he thought he had probably witnessed the end of the temporal power of the Dalai Lama.

Before the close of 1908, the Dalai Lama left Peking to return to Lhasa. During the next few years the Chinese were to find that the "Most Excellent, Self-existent Buddha of the West" had a more rebellious spirit than is ordinarily associated with divinity. When Chinese troops approached Lhasa in February, 1910, the Dalai Lama fled to Darjeeling in India, and China found it difficult to maintain order among the rebellious Tibetans. When China was beset by revolution in 1912, these tribesmen overwhelmed the Chinese garrison and the Dalai Lama returned to govern.

During these hectic years he continued to seek the advice of Rockhill, addressing him as "the American Minister, the great dignitary, whose knowledge and whose virtues are as great as the heavens." Rockhill consistently advised the Dalai Lama that he should seek to establish good relations with China, that only in this way could Tibet have good government.

Not until 1951 was agreement between China and Tibet reached, although there were two important attempts at settlement, once in 1914 and again in 1921. Tibet claimed independence after 1913. When the Chinese failed to recognize this claim and pointed to the Chinese support of the lamaseries, the Dalai Lama replied that a priest does not become the property of laymen

[16] Rockhill to Roosevelt, November 8, 1908, Rockhill Papers in the possession of Miss Crutch.

[17] Rockhill made detailed notes of his dealings with the Dalai Lama; these are included in the Rockhill Papers in the possession of Miss Crutch.

simply because he has accepted their aid. This spirit of defiance on the part of the Dalai Lama was made possible by existing conditions in China.

Civil and foreign wars prevented China's establishing effective control, but, during the summer of 1950, the new Communist regime in China threatened to march an army of 100,000 into Tibet. The prospect of a Communist state along its 2,000 mile border created uneasiness in India, and that country now took the place of Great Britain as the advocate of Tibetan autonomy. Tibet, however, received no effective support. On May 27, 1951, Tibet yielded to Chinese Communist pressure, surrendering her sovereignty and agreeing to the absorption of her small army into that of China.

CHAPTER ELEVEN

A New Post and a New Diplomacy

A vice-consul, present during one of Rockhill's visits to Hankow, wrote that he was more than ever impressed with the particularly high regard the Chinese had for the American Minister. He observed that "with his [Rockhill's] knowledge of the language, people, and the country, official China everywhere extends to him such treatment, which for frankness, sincerity and respect, has heretofore never been surpassed." [1] The farewell dinner given Rockhill by China's Foreign Office, an event reported as unprecedented, showed fully the Chinese respect and admiration for Rockhill and their appreciation for his interest in them. When his final day as Minister arrived, Rockhill sadly noted: "Can my work with China be at an end? I pray that it be not terminated entirely."

Shortly after the election of William Howard Taft, Rockhill, in accordance with the traditions of the foreign service, offered his resignation to the President-elect and stated that he would be glad to stay or serve in some other place. If he was to be transferred, he wrote, he would prefer Constantinople.[2] When President Taft appointed him Ambassador to Russia in April, 1909, both Rockhill and his friends expressed surprise. Henry Adams queried: "Rockhill's promotion quite agitated us, but it is made more perplexing by wonder how he can live. He can't!" [3]

Hippisley, visiting in Baltimore, reported that the American newspaper press attributed the appointment to his "special aptitude" in dealing with questions likely to arise in connection with Manchuria.[4] This was verified by William Phillips, Rockhill's most intimate friend in the Department of State, who informed him: "I know that, personally, you preferred Constantinople, but I think you will be complimented to hear the reasons why the Secretary wished you to go to Petersburg. He believes that by far the most important post and where we have real problems to overcome." A generous rent allowance was provided to make it possible for Rockhill to accept.[5]

---

[1] Albert W. Pontius to the Assistant Secretary of State Robert Bacon, April 12, 1908, Department of State Archives.

[2] W. W. Rockhill to President William Howard Taft, November 5, 1908, Department of State Archives.

[3] *Henry Adams and His Friends: A Collection of His Unpublished Letters*, ed. Harold Dean Cater (Boston: Houghton Mifflin Co., 1947), p. 655.

[4] Alfred E. Hippisley to Rockhill, June 2, 1909, Rockhill Papers.

[5] William Phillips to Rockhill, April 27, 1909, Rockhill Papers.

Ideally suited for the post in Peking, Rockhill, according to the State Department policy of frequent transfer, should have been equally well qualified to represent the United States at St. Petersburg. Yet Rockhill knew little or nothing about the Czarist Empire; the most that can be said for the appointment is that he had an understanding of the Far Eastern problems on which Taft and Knox hoped to secure Russia's cooperation, and that he was an experienced diplomat.

The new policy of Taft and Knox was as strange to Rockhill as his new post. He had been trained in the old school of diplomacy where foreign policy was less the shield of the Republic than the instrument for aiding commercial and religious interests. During his earlier diplomatic career, Rockhill had concerned himself chiefly with protecting the treaty rights of Americans in China to carry on business and missionary work. The Open Door notes with their emphasis on markets for American goods symbolized the limited aims of the old diplomacy. Only insofar as Rockhill had sought to make the Open Door a policy for protecting the integrity of China had he departed from the traditional policy.

With the Taft administration, a new diplomacy, embodying far-reaching aims and employing new methods, came into being. Hitherto business interests largely shaped foreign policy; now business became a weapon of the nation state for achieving more ambitious goals. The transition was not sudden and not original with the Taft administration but now for the first time in American history it became policy.

This new policy, dubbed "dollar diplomacy" by its opponents, was inspired by Willard Straight. Upon his graduation from Cornell in 1901, Straight had gone to China to work for the Imperial Chinese Maritime Customs Service. During the Russo-Japanese War he joined the foreign service of the United States and served as Vice-Consul at Seoul and later as Consul-General at Mukden in Manchuria. Distressed by Japanese domination in that area, he saw the possibility of counteracting the Japanese by building up American investments. Apparently the first encouragement he received came from the representatives of two British and French syndicates who had been guests at the consulate. They informed Straight that their companies, unlike their governments, wished to call a halt to the Japanese advance. He told the State Department that: "Both believe that it should be possible for American, British and French financiers to create a community of interests which would minimize the danger, which they regard as imminent, that Japan will attempt to secure and exercise for her exclusive benefit, domination in the Three Eastern Provinces, or, at least, the central and southern portions thereof." [6]

Straight failed to see the significance of the fact that neither the British nor French governments would support such a drive against the Japanese. He saw only the offer of cooperation by foreign capitalists and an opportunity for his own

---

[6] Willard Straight to Bacon, September 28, 1907, Department of State Archives.

government to take the lead in stopping Japan. His enthusiasm led him to overlook the hazards of such a diplomatic venture.

When Rockhill received his appointment to go to Russia in April, 1909, Straight was already Chief of the Far Eastern Division in the Department of State and the policy he had outlined in September, 1907, was taking shape. During his last weeks in Peking, Rockhill received instructions to take a strong stand in favor of American participation in the financing and construction of the Hukuang railways in central China. The British, French, and German capitalists were about to complete negotiations when Straight pushed for action. He noted in his diary: "Telegram sent to Peking which started the row about the Chinese loan. Bill [William Phillips?] tried to ask a question merely, but with H. W. [Huntington Wilson] approving, my telegram went, telling Rockhill, if press reports were true, to take immediate action." [7]

Rockhill, although having no knowledge that this was the first step in a program to make American business the handmaiden of the State Department for the purpose of playing a major role in the Far East, dutifully called on the Foreign Office three times to press for American participation. The reply he received did not indicate that China was eager to have the United States expand its interests as a counterpoise to Japan. Rockhill could only relay the most evasive answers to the Secretary of State.[8]

Rockhill returned to the United States in June, 1909, for conferences in Washington. It may be assumed that he learned something of the new zeal which had invaded the State Department, but the daring strategy to be employed had not yet been worked out when he left for Russia. The new Secretary of State, Philander C. Knox, having had no experience in foreign affairs, found it necessary to devote several months to a study of past policy before outlining a program.

In June, 1909, Straight left his post at the State Department to become the representative of a newly organized group of American bankers composed of J. P. Morgan, Kuhn, Loeb, and Company, The First National Bank of New York, the National City Bank of New York, and Edward H. Harriman. This combination of financial interests had been organized by the State Department for the purpose of gaining entry into the proposed Hukuang railroad system. En route to Peking, Straight conferred with French, German, and British bankers who were meeting in London to discuss, among other things, what share the Americans should have in the Hukuang railroads. Next he went to France, where Harriman was in the midst of negotiations with Russian agents for the purchase of the Chinese Eastern Railway. Fearing that the Russians might not agree to sell their railroad in northern Manchuria, Harriman instructed Straight

[7] Willard Straight's diary, entry May 24, 1909; cited by Herbert Croly, *Willard Straight* (New York: Macmillan Co., 1924), p. 282.

[8] Rockhill to Secretary of State Philander Knox, June 1, 1909, Department of State Archives.

to seek a contract from the Chinese for the building of a north-south railroad from Chinchow to Aigun. This line would parallel the Chinese Eastern Railway and could be used as a bargaining point with the Russians. Then even if they refused to sell the Chinese Eastern, the Americans would be in possession of a contract for a railroad of considerable economic importance. Harriman and Straight agreed that the success of the Manchurian railway venture depended on securing Russian cooperation.

In line with his conversations with Harriman, Straight wrote to Knox expressing hope that the United States might gain Russia's political support for enterprises in northern Manchuria and Mongolia "in return for a little financial 'face' for the Russo-Chinese Bank." [9] Mindful of Rockhill's more traditional view of diplomacy, Straight dropped a warning: "In this connection by the way, unless our friend Rockhill has been well chastened, our hold at Petersburg will not be an overstrong one."

Early in October, Straight was successful in negotiating a preliminary agreement with the Chinese Viceroy in Manchuria for the Chinchow-Aigun line. This action coincided with a final formulation of policy by Secretary Knox. On October 8, he outlined his conclusions in a letter to his close friend, Henry M. Hoyt, a counsellor for the Department of State. He proposed the following principle in dealing with railway questions in China: "In all cases where the Imperial credit of China is pledged for railway construction, the Powers which have pledged themselves to the principle of equal trade opportunities in China and the preservation of China's political integrity have such a direct interest as to entitle them to participation in the loans and equitable consideration for their nationals and materials." [10] Knox also maintained that exclusive rights should not be granted to do business within the territory served by a railroad which had been constructed upon imperial credit or pledge of provincial revenues.[11]

The policy which Knox proposed went far beyond anything laid down in the Hay notes of 1899. At that time, Rockhill had advised that it was hopeless to ask for equality of opportunity in the field of railroad construction. Knox's conclusions calling for a broadening of the Open Door policy to cover railroad investments reflected Straight's opinion that railroads furnished the key to the development of a market for American goods in Manchuria. The loss of this market after the Russo-Japanese War had caused endless complaints by American merchants and both Taft and Knox were interested in helping them.

In the fall of 1909, evidence of Russian readiness to cooperate with the United States was not lacking. In the spring of 1907, Fred D. Fisher, the American Consul at Harbin, had reported that negotiations were under way with a Belgian syndicate for the sale of the railroad. In July of the same year,

[9] Straight to Knox, August 3, 1909, Department of State Archives.

[10] Knox to Henry M. Hoyt, October 8, 1909, Knox Papers, Library of Congress.

[11] *Ibid.*

Fisher forwarded information that some of the railway clerks had not been paid for three months and that the railroad was enormously in debt.[12] In the summer of 1908, Russian Minister of Finance Kokovstev and Foreign Minister Isvolsky had reached a decision to sell the Chinese Eastern Railway to an international syndicate providing Japan would sell the South Manchurian Railway.[13] Accordingly, an agent of the Minister of Finance, Willenkin, approached Kuhn, Loeb, and Company.[14] Negotiations were dropped when the Japanese refused to consider the project. It was known that the Russian Minister of Finance favored selling to Harriman in the summer of 1909.[15] Harriman died in September, shortly after his conversations with Straight, and the project was then taken over by the Department of State. During October, Rockhill's reports encouraged the Secretary to believe that it was by no means futile to hope that Russia would go along with him on the project of neutralization.[16]

Despite the economic considerations favoring the sale of the road, it must be recognized that both Russia and Japan had footholds in Manchuria which their vital interests in that area would not permit them to surrender. In the case of Japan, with the privileges which she had gained in Manchuria as a result of her recent war with Russia, it was even less likely that she would accept the Knox proposal, the aim of which was to reduce her position to the same as that of other nations. It was not so obvious that Russia would prove recalcitrant. Russia faced an acute situation in Manchuria owing to increased Japanese pressure during the summer of 1909. To Knox it seemed that his neutralization proposal provided Russia with a dignified way of escape. So convinced was Knox of the desirability of his scheme from the Russian point of view that he made no concessions to Russia on the Harbin question although at that time the issue was serving as a major irritant in relations between the two countries.[17]

---

[12] Fred D. Fisher to Rockhill, July 6, 1907, Department of State Archives.

[13] Edward H. Zabriskie, *American-Russian Rivalry in the Far East: A Study in Diplomacy and Power Politics, 1895-1914* (Philadelphia: University of Pennsylvania Press, 1946), pp. 149-50.

[14] *Ibid.;* Croly, *op. cit.*, pp. 278-79.

[15] Zabriskie, *op. cit.*, p. 154; Croly, *op. cit.*, p. 310.

[16] Rockhill to Knox, October 25, 1909, Department of State Archives.

[17] In January, 1908, Russia established a municipal administration in Harbin, the northern terminus of the Chinese Eastern Railway. The Czar's government, replying to protests of China and the United States, defended its action on the basis of the concession granted to the Chinese Eastern Railway Company in 1896. The United States not only denied the Russian interpretation of the terms of the concession but held that Russia's action in Harbin constituted a violation of the Treaty of Portsmouth wherein she had agreed to uphold the Open Door and respect China's sovereignty. Although Russia and China reached an agreement in May, 1909, the United States continued to make periodic protests and Americans in Harbin were instructed not to pay taxes to the municipal administration or to recognize its authority in any way.

If the evidence of Russian willingness to sell the Chinese Eastern Railway was inconclusive, the Secretary of State was quite aware of this fact and also aware that the negotiations might lead to a Russian-Japanese rapprochement. On October 30, 1909, Henry Fletcher, Chargé d'Affaires at Peking, cabled that he thought the visit to the Far East of Kokovstev, Russian Minister of Finance, and a speech given at Dalny by Prince Ito of Japan, pointed to the two countries reaching an understanding in the near future in regard to Manchuria. On November 2, Fletcher cabled that he had discussed the Harbin question with Korostovetz, Russian Minister at Peking, and that he "seemed to intimate that the continued opposition of the foreign Powers to Russian policy in Manchuria might drive them to make common cause with Japan."

Secretary Knox also expected that Great Britain and France would join the United States in supporting the neutralization of Manchurian railroads. He failed to recognize that the alliances which these two countries had with Russia and Japan would make them reluctant to exert pressure in behalf of his proposal. Whether Rockhill had much hope of British and French support is uncertain. His first-hand experience after the Boxer revolt—when Great Britain and France had sacrificed their Far Eastern interests to strengthening their positions in Europe—should have made him sceptical of receiving their support.

Although American diplomats in 1909 too readily assumed that Great Britain and France would support neutralization, they recognized the possibility of Russia joining hands with Japan. In the diplomatic correspondence of the closing months of the year, fear of this was frequently expressed; they realized the dangers but decided that there were enough favorable factors to warrant their taking the chance.

On his arrival in St. Petersburg in October, Ambassador Rockhill reported that the Russians were very apprehensive about a recent agreement between China and Japan, and it looked as if they might seek the cooperation of the United States in order to counteract Japanese influence.[18] More important in view of the plans being drawn in the State Department was Rockhill's statement that an official high in the Ministry of Finance had said that a project was under way for the sale of the Chinese Eastern Railway.[19]

As yet neither Rockhill nor the Department of State was aware that the Ministry of Finance, looking at the railroad question from a profit and loss point of view, might not find its plans approved by the Ministry of Foreign Affairs, which was less influenced by business factors than by broader national considerations. Therefore, when Foreign Minister Isvolsky told Rockhill that the policy of Russia was to strengthen China, it was easy to link the statements of the two departments and to assume that the project about to be launched would gain Russia's approval.

[18] Rockhill to Knox, October 19, 1909, Department of State Archives.

[19] *Ibid.*, November 19, 1909.

On November 6, Secretary Knox sent to Ambassador Rockhill a confidential memorandum of a plan for the neutralization. It consisted of two parts. The first called for the establishment of an international syndicate to aid China in buying the Chinese Eastern and the South Manchurian railways. The second part of the proposal, stated as an alternative, was an invitation to Russia and Japan to participate in the financing and construction of the Chinchow-Aigun railway.[20] Rockhill noted in his diary: "Got interesting tel. from D. of S. [Department of State] on neutralization of Manchu R.R. A good scheme if it can be carried through." [21] It was on this ambitious plan that Knox based his hopes for a fuller realization of the Open Door. Rockhill may or may not have foreseen the difficulties ahead, but his reports encouraged the Department.

In his instruction to Rockhill accompanying the confidential memorandum, Secretary Knox stated:

> The Government of the United States is gratified at the statement of the Russian Minister for Foreign Affairs that the policy Russia [*sic*] is to strengthen China. It seems clear to me that you have now a rare opportunity to further our policies by making shrewd and discreet use, as if the ideas originated with yourself, of the fundamental ideas put before the Embassy in previous telegrams and notably in that of November sixth which quotes confidentially the Memorandum to be handed to the British Government. You will find yourself free to foster the idea of Russian cooperation in neutralizing the railroads of Manchuria by joining with us, Great Britain and other interested governments supporting the open door. . . .[22]

The instruction closed on an ominous note which shows that Secretary Knox was not unmindful of the dangers involved. He urged Rockhill to "seek to forestall any arrangement between Russia and Japan contrary in spirit to the project of the complete commercial neutralization of Manchuria." [23]

Rockhill explained the Knox plan to Foreign Minister Isvolsky, emphasizing the advantages to be gained. Isvolsky, cool and sceptical, thought it would weaken the military position of Russia and expressed the belief that Japan's consent could not be secured without coercion. He asked for a confidential memorandum.[24] In his diary, however, Rockhill noted that he thought Isvolsky liked the scheme in principle.

Rockhill made no mention of the Chinchow-Aigun agreement, although he was convinced that the American position would be strengthened by informing the Russians of the British and American preliminary agreement with the Imperial government to finance and build the new railway in Manchuria. Rockhill telegraphed Secretary Knox asking permission to do so.[25] The Secretary of State

[20] Knox to Rockhill, November 6, 1909, Department of State Archives.

[21] Rockhill's diary, entry November 10, 1909, Rockhill Papers.

[22] Knox to Rockhill, November 10, 1909, Rockhill Papers.

[23] *Ibid.*

[24] Rockhill to Knox, November 13, 1909, Department of State Archives.

[25] *Ibid.*

thought this information should be withheld until the British (already in possession of Knox's memorandum) had given their views on the neutralization proposal. He instructed Rockhill that he might refer to press reports that such a concession had been granted.[26]

The realization of the Knox plan depended to a large extent on the cooperation of Russia. This was recognized by the Secretary, and consequently, in December and January, the efforts made to win over Russia were greater than those made to gain Japanese acceptance.

When Rockhill formally presented the neutralization proposal in December in an *aide-memoire,* Isvolsky expressed disappointment over the general nature of the plan but promised to give it careful consideration.[27] Again Rockhill made no reference to the Chinchow-Aigun agreement. When he interviewed Isvolsky on December 25, the Foreign Minister, who had now learned of the alternative proposal from reports received from the Russian embassies in London and Tokyo, expressed surprise that information had been withheld from Russia while it had been given out to others. The American Ambassador, obviously embarrassed by this omission, cabled the Secretary of State:

> Minister for Foreign Affairs informed me yesterday afternoon that he has been advised Memorandum presented by some of our diplomatic representatives on the subject neutralization Manchuria railroads contains the text of the alternative proposal and that the statement is made in it that the contract for the Chinchow-Aigun railroad has been concluded. In view of your telegrams November 13, 6:00 p.m. and December 15, 4:00 p.m. the Embassy did not include the alternative proposal in the memorandum handed Minister for Foreign Affairs, although a general *great antipathy* to scheme agreeing with it had been orally discussed with him a short time ago. Shall I inform him of the alternative proposal in full? Can I say that contract has been perfected and the United States and Great Britain will support it diplomatically? [28]

Knox replied:

> It was the intention of the Department that you communicate to the Russian Foreign Office a paraphrase of the full text of the memorandum contained in the telegram of November sixth, omitting, as a matter of propriety, only the reference to the secret edict in the opening paragraph.
>
> You need not conceal the fact that the contract for the Chinchow-Aigun line has been signed and will be supported diplomatically by the United States and Great Britain.[29]

In a memorandum to the Russian Ambassador in Washington, Knox attributed the omission to Rockhill's misunderstanding of the instructions.[30]

---

[26] Knox to Rockhill, November 16, 1909, Department of State Archives.

[27] Montgomery Schuyler to Knox, December 20, 1909, Department of State Archives.

[28] Rockhill to Knox, December 26, 1909, Department of State Archives.

[29] Knox to Rockhill, December 27, 1909, Department of State Archives.

[30] Knox memorandum to Russian Embassy, February 8, 1910, Department of State Archives. The instruction of December 15, 1909, read: "In presenting Memorandum to For-

On December 27, Rockhill called on Isvolsky again and gave him another memorandum stating the advantages to be gained by Russia if the neutralization proposal were adopted. Isvolsky was now openly hostile. Rockhill noted in his diary: "I had a heated conversation of an hour with Isvolsky, but it amounted to nothing. For some unknown reason he likes to lash himself into a fury with me." [31]

During January, Rockhill continued to seek Isvolsky's approval of the Knox plan but received no encouragement. According to Pourtales, German Ambassador at St. Petersburg, Rockhill, as late as January 12, was of the opinion that the Russians were considering the Knox neutralization scheme. In an interview with Isvolsky, Rockhill had met each of the Foreign Minister's objections. Isvolsky had expressed fear of a powerful China to which Rockhill had replied that a strong China would make for peace in the Far East and that it was Japan, with its excess population forcing it to adopt an aggressive policy, which constituted the real danger. When Isvolsky had raised the specter of an alliance between China and Japan, the Ambassador stated that the traditional enmity and distrust between the two made this unlikely.[32]

While he continued to seek Russia's acceptance of Secretary Knox's plan, Rockhill was greatly disturbed by Knox's persistence in pressing the Czar's government on the Harbin question. Late in December, Rockhill wrote that the troublesome Harbin question "is causing me great anxiety as it is creating pronounced bitterness in the Minister for Foreign Affairs and prejudices him in consideration of other matters connected with China." [33] Since early in 1908,

---

eign Office omit as a matter of propriety written reference to unpublished edict which however was authenticated by definite statement made to Straight by Grand Councilor." Rockhill understood this to mean that Russia should be given no information concerning the Chinchow-Aigun arrangement. In reaching this decision he was influenced by an earlier instruction (in reply to his suggestion that Russia be informed of the agreement) stating that it would not be proper to notify Russia until Great Britain had replied to the proposal. While there may have been some justification for the misunderstanding, the author is of the opinion that Rockhill must be charged with an error.

Rockhill's mistake helped to create ill feeling on the part of Foreign Minister Isvolsky who felt that the United States had slighted his country which had a greater interest in Manchuria than most of the powers who had been notified. The aim of American diplomacy had been to gain Russia's support, thereby making it more difficult for Japan to reject the neutralization proposal. Yet it appears unlikely that this was the cause of failure. Isvolsky had indicated but slight sympathy previous to Rockhill's error, and appears to have been so convinced of the necessity for cooperating with Japan, who was a military menace to the maritime provinces, that the Knox plan had no chance of success as long as he held office.

[31] Rockhill's diary, entry December 27, 1909, Rockhill Papers.

[32] Count Friedrich von Pourtales to Bethmann-Hollweg, January 12, 1910, *Di Grosse Politik,* XXXII, pp. 76-77.

[33] Rockhill to Knox, December 29, 1909, Department of State Archives.

the United States had been protesting against Russia's establishment of a municipal administration at Harbin. Rather than drop the question, Knox reasoned that if the protests were continued Russia would see in his neutralization scheme a way out of the Harbin difficulty. Instead, Knox's protests only predisposed Isvolsky to reject the proposal of the United States. Not until the middle of January did Rockhill succeed in convincing Knox of the advisability of postponing discussion of Harbin. Even then Knox merely agreed that Americans in Harbin might pay taxes to the municipal administration with the understanding that the whole question might be submitted to an international court for settlement. While Knox might have been cultivating good relations with the Czar's Foreign Minister, he was, instead, irritating him by futile protests on an issue of lesser importance.

Reports from London and Tokyo early in January indicated that both Russia and Japan would reject the Knox proposal.[34] On January 21, the Czar's government presented Rockhill with its formal reply. Isvolsky explained that Russia saw no threat to the Open Door policy in Manchuria and therefore believed that there was no need for a reconsideration of the question raised by the United States. The adoption of the proposal "would seriously injure Russian interests, both public and private, to which the Imperial Government attaches a capital importance." Concerning the Chinchow-Aigun line, Isvolsky observed that it affected Russian interests vitally and had political and strategic significance.[35]

In forwarding the Russian reply to the Knox proposal, Rockhill reported: "The comments of the press are distinctly divided along purely political lines, the government and conservative organs being opposed to the general proposal, the liberal press in favor of it; while both are disposed to favor a fuller consideration of the question of Russian participation in the Chinchow-Aigun Railway." [36]

Quite as disturbing as the rejection of the neutralization proposal was the report that Russia and Japan had conferred before preparing their replies.[37] Russian and Japanese collaboration was also indicated by the fact that both had notified the United States on January 21. Three days after receiving the Russian *aide-memoire,* Rockhill wrote to the Secretary of State stating again that he had reliable information that the Russian government was in constant communication with Japan during the drafting of the reply. While he was of the opinion that

[34] American Ambassador O'Brien in Tokyo reported that Count Komura, Minister for Foreign Affairs, seemed opposed. O'Brien to Knox, December 24, 1909, Department of State Archives.

Phillips cabled from London: "Reports from Tokyo and St. Petersburg received by Foreign Office appear to indicate that neither Russia nor Japan looked with favor upon proposal for neutralization of existing Manchurian railways." William Phillips to Knox, January 6, 1910, Department of State Archives.

[35] Rockhill to Knox, January 21, 1910, Department of State Archives.

[36] *Ibid.,* January 22, 1910.

[37] *Ibid.*

there would be no alliance between Russia and Japan, Rockhill thought nothing could be more dangerous for the peace of the Far East.[38]

What Rockhill feared had already happened. Edward H. Zabriskie, in *American-Russian Rivalry in the Far East,* draws upon Russian sources to show that Isvolsky considered the neutralization proposal inadequate protection for Russian interests in the Amur region in the face of the strong military position of Japan. On November 13, the same day that Rockhill presented the Knox proposal informally, Baron Motono of Japan, offered Isvolsky an alliance which assured him of Japanese support on the Harbin question and security for the maritime provinces in the event of war in Europe. The Russian Foreign Minister, easily convinced of the desirability of accepting the Japanese proposal, had to convert Czar Nicholas II, who had leaned strongly toward the American project. Isvolsky had no trouble in so doing; it remained only to work out the phraseology of the negative reply to be given to Rockhill.

The United States, including Rockhill, had been given a lesson in the realities of international power politics. Russian and Japanese capital in Manchuria was but an instrument for carrying out basic national aims. If the United States wished to counter those aims and to protect what it conceived to be its own interests in that area, it must be willing to pay a greater price than any which could be measured in dollars.

On January 20, Secretary Knox, in a last minute effort to stave off defeat, had telegraphed the American Ambassador at St. Petersburg that the United States would appreciate an opportunity to present "a fuller explanation of certain matters directly bearing upon the question." Rockhill did not receive this dispatch until January 23, after the Russian reply. When he asked for the opportunity to present additional explanations, the Russians ignored the neutralization proposal and merely replied that further information on the Chinchow-Aigun proposal would be received with pleasure.[39] On February 8, Knox presented a further explanation but it received scant attention. The discussions on the Chinchow-Aigun proposal were now transferred to Washington where Knox found the Russians no more inclined to adopt his views.

When the vital interests of nations clash, it is easy to personalize the blame, and, in 1910, when Russia rejected the Knox proposals, Isvolsky became the target of American criticism. Rockhill, disillusioned with his treatment at the hands of Isvolsky, wrote to E. T. Williams, in the Division of Far Eastern Affairs, expressing an intention to resign.[40] So great was the inclination in Washington to blame Isvolsky for the failure that the State Department naively contemplated seeking his removal from office. In a letter to Rockhill, Mont-

[38] *Ibid.,* January 24, 1910.

[39] *Ibid.,* January 29, 1910.

[40] In reply to a letter written January 12, E. T. Williams wrote: "I have kept your letter entirely confidential, as you requested. My inquiries therefore have been limited to the

gomery Schuyler, who had recently returned to Washington from the American Embassy at St. Petersburg, wrote:

The Far Eastern Division wants you to understand that the Department proposes to back you up *absolutely* in the whole Manchurian matter. Both Mr. Miller and Mr. Wilson know Isvolsky personally and consider him capable of anything unfriendly to the United States. Your memoranda of Dec. 31st and my conference (with Mr. Wilson and Mr. Calhoun) brought this out still more forcibly. The Dept. looks for no improvement in Russo-American relations until Isvolsky is entirely "eliminated" from the situation. This they were about to attempt themselves until I arrived on the scene and urged caution, delay and less far reaching steps. I thought it best to advise against the dispatch to you of a telegram instructing you to ask for an immediate audience with the Emperor to complain of I's attitude toward the U.S. and I drafted the instructions saying that it might be necessary to ask for an audience. I should be against too active steps to "remove" I.[41]

Isvolsky continued to oppose American plans in Manchuria. The Chinchow-Aigun proposal, approved by a Chinese imperial edict on January 21, 1910, met with Russian suggestions that the route be altered, and Russia took the position that her approval was necessary before any final decision could be taken by the United States.[42] Secretary Knox strongly denied that Russian consent was necessary before Americans could proceed.[43] No progress was made, and the Chinchow-Aigun project failed to materialize.

Mankind's willingness to repeat a lesson even after the proverbial fingers have been scorched was well illustrated by the State Department after it had been rebuffed in its neutralization scheme. On September 22, 1910, China approached the United States for a loan of 50,000,000 *taels* to carry out currency reform. On October 2, the Chinese increased the amount of the loan requested to $50,000,000 in order to provide funds for the development of Manchuria.[44] The American bankers had been extremely reluctant to continue as financial agent of the Department of State because of the international complications which had developed and only the urging of Secretary Knox held them.[45] On October 27, their agent in Peking signed a preliminary agreement.

---

report that Mr. O'Brien was inclined to leave Tokyo. I can find no confirmation here at all of such a desire upon his part. He has apparently not mentioned it here, or, if he did, it was not taken seriously. . . .

"I trust you will not think of resigning. You are too much needed in the service and opportunity for a transfer may occur at any time. I sympathize with your desire to get back to the Orient, and hope it may be gratified. You are so well equipped for the Far East and understand the oriental mind so well that an exchange with Tokyo, to my thinking, would be a fine thing." E. T. Williams to Rockhill, February 8, 1910, Rockhill Papers.

[41] Montgomery Schuyler to Rockhill, February 15, 1910, Department of State Archives.

[42] Rockhill to Knox, January 21, 1910, Department of State Archives.

[43] Memorandum from Knox to Russian Embassy, February 14, 1910, Department of State Archives.

[44] W. J. Calhoun to Knox, October 2, 1910, Department of State Archives.

[45] Croly, *op. cit.*, pp. 341-44.

This provided that the American bankers might have associates but that the final agreement should be signed with Americans alone. The type of security to be offered was not specified.[46] These two questions led to complications strikingly similar to those fostered by the Knox neutralization proposal.

Willard Straight, on his way to Peking to represent the American bankers, stopped at St. Petersburg to discuss the loan with Rockhill. Straight's aggressiveness as American Consul at Mukden had caused disagreement between the two, but relations had become cordial since that time. Straight wrote:

> I found him a most charming man, as I always knew I should once I was no longer his subordinate. I didn't have it out, but I shall some day, and I think we shall be very good friends. I am quite willing to admit my own unruliness, but I insist that he did not stand for progress. Had he had his way we would never have been where we are, but since we are here, I am all for taking his advice to proceed carefully and conservatively. We must now try to fortify ourselves in a position which we have attained by rather daring means.[47]

The "daring means" Straight employed scarcely strengthened the diplomatic position of the United States. Straight evidently confused activity with success, and Rockhill knew it. He cautioned Straight that Russian support for the currency loan should be enlisted from the outset.[48]

During the winter of 1910-1911, the representatives of the four-power consortium of bankers carried on negotiations with the Peking authorities. The Manchu-Chinese officials objected to joint signatories and to having a foreign adviser who would have the power to control expenditures of the loan funds. Straight, representing the American bankers, encountered strong resistance; but on April 15, 1911, the final agreement was signed. It provided for joint signatories, and, if the European bankers objected to having an American as adviser, an adviser of some nationality not interested in loans to China should be appointed. Article XVI provided that if China should need further loans for completing the operations contemplated in the agreement, the banks participating in the currency loan should be the first invited to furnish such funds.[49]

The foreign offices of Russia and Japan, as well as those of Great Britain, Germany, and France, had been notified of the preliminary agreement and had been invited to participate on October 31, 1910. British, German, and French bankers immediately requested participation. The foreign offices of Russia and Japan failed to reply; they viewed the international loan for the reform of China's currency and the industrial development of Manchuria as another version of Secretary Knox's neutralization scheme.

---

[46] Calhoun to Knox, October 27, 1910, Department of State Archives.

[47] Straight to Dorothy Whitney, November [?], 1910; cited by Croly, *op. cit.*, p. 366.

[48] Straight to Rockhill, December 11, 1910, Rockhill Papers.

[49] Calhoun to Knox, April 27, 1911, Department of State Archives.

American "dollar diplomacy" practically forced Russia and Japan to seek protection of their interests in Manchuria and Mongolia. Russia charged that the Chinese were guilty of violations of their treaty of 1881. On March 16, Rockhill informed Secretary Knox that Russia insisted "upon full and absolute compliance within a limited period. . . ." Rockhill also reported that the Japanese Ambassador had told him that the situation was extremely serious, that Japan had urged Peking to comply with the Russian demands, and that he hoped the American government would advise Peking to the same effect.[50] Before the end of March, American Minister Calhoun in Peking cabled that China had yielded completely to the Russian demands.[51]

Opposition to the currency loan appeared early in 1911. On January 30, Rockhill warned Secretary Knox that Russian cooperation was necessary to success. Russia had possessions and interests in northern Asia incomparably greater and more vital than those of any other Western power. The fact that Russian frontiers touched those of Japan, and were contiguous for thousands of miles with those of China, made it certain that Russia could never withdraw from participation in Far Eastern affairs.

> With the exception of Japan and China herself, no other Power is similarly interested in those dominions of China with the fate of which American policy is immediately concerned. In the case of every other European power, Far Eastern questions are in fact wholly subordinated to considerations of purely European politics. . . . Except casually and occasionally, therefore, our Government can reckon upon no European support in the maintenance of those principles of Chinese integrity and the open door in the northern dominions of China, which are potentially threatened by Russia in Mongolia and by Russia and Japan in Manchuria.[52]

In conclusion, Rockhill expressed the opinion that while Russian policy was not aggressive but precautionary, Japan had "an almost immediate need of expansion upon the mainland of Asia." [53] He was not aware that, at a meeting of the Russian Council of Ministers on December 2, it had been agreed that ultimate annexation of northern Manchuria was a necessity.[54]

Evidence of Russian opposition to the currency loan was not long in forthcoming. On April 24, Rockhill forwarded an editorial from the *Novoe Vremya,* a newspaper expressing the views of the Russian Foreign Office, stating that the loan aimed at strengthening Chinese opposition to Russian and Japanese

[50] Rockhill to Knox, March 16, 1911, Department of State Archives.

[51] Calhoun to Knox, March 29, 1911, Department of State Archives.

[52] Memorandum of Russian relations with the United States prepared by J. V. A. MacMurray, June 3, 1911, contains Rockhill's dispatch to Secretary Knox, January 30, 1911, Rockhill Papers.

[53] *Ibid.*

[54] B. De Siebert, *Entente Diplomacy and the World: Matrix of the History of Europe, 1909-1914,* trans. by G. A. Schreiner (New York: G. P. Putnam's Sons, 1921), p. 23.

claims in Manchuria.[55] On May 13, Acting Foreign Minister Neratoff informed Rockhill that Russia and Japan were exchanging views as to the effect of the currency loan on their interests in Manchuria.[56] Secretary Knox, hoping to eliminate Russian suspicion, dispatched a statement of policy repeating that the American government was actuated by hope "of preserving for the common benefit of all nations the commercial possibilities of China and its dominions." [57]

On July 11, Russia and Japan protested against Article XVI. Referring to this article, the Russian note stated:

> Such a stipulation creates in favor of the syndicate mentioned a preferential position in Manchuria. It seems that the syndicate pretends to a monopoly of financial and industrial enterprises in the region in which Russia possesses important special interests. The Imperial Government has always respected the right belonging to the other nations in Manchuria, and for its part holds that there should be no disregard of its legitimate rights acquired in that country. Now, the project in question having a tendency to hinder the development of Russian interests in Manchuria by creating in favor of the syndicate an altogether exceptional position, the Imperial Government earnestly hopes that consideration will be given to the objections formulated above, and addresses itself to the Government of the United States with the request that it will not refuse to use its influence with a view to having clause 16 of the contract revoked.[58]

Rockhill, who had been granted his request for a transfer to Constantinople, cabled from Geneva that he had not considered it expedient to communicate the text of Secretary Knox's statement of policy because the Minister for Foreign Affairs was absent from the capital. He had discussed the statement with Minister of Finance Kokovstev who had not concealed "dislike of recent currency loan which excluding as he said the two powers with preponderating interests in Manchuria did not harmonize with our professions." [59]

Efforts were made to meet the Russian and Japanese objections. Willard Straight returned to Peking to carry out further negotiations. However, the outbreak of revolution in China, on October 10, 1911, brought an end to the negotiations and to the hopes of Knox and Straight. Their efforts to make the Open Door policy effective had failed. In view of the strong opposition by Russia and Japan, it seems likely that the loan was destined to failure even before the revolution.

Rockhill was pleased when his request for a transfer to Constantinople was granted in June. His career in St. Petersburg was marked by no diplomatic success. While visiting his mother in Geneva, Switzerland, prior to assuming his new post, he wrote to Hippisley:

---

[55] Rockhill to Knox, April 24, 1911, Department of State Archives.

[56] *Ibid.*, May 13, 1911.

[57] Knox to Rockhill, June 7, 1911, Rockhill Papers.

[58] Prince N. Koudacheff to Knox, July 11, 1911, Department of State Archives.

[59] Rockhill to Knox, July 21, 1911, Rockhill Papers.

Thanks for your congratulations on my appointment to Constantinople. I am delighted to go there—it is again the East and it is much easier—cheaper—to live there than in Russia. I hated being obliged to be constantly on the alert to make both ends meet. As to my value to the Govt. in the post of St. Petersburg, the people in Washington have their own ideas as to the way of carrying out our present policy (?) in the Far East, they do not want or care for my views on things Chinese. They understand them much better than I do. Personally I think we are making a miserable mess of things in China and instead of being—as we might leaders—we are led, so I am glad I am out of it.[60]

[60] Rockhill to Hippisley, July [?], 1911, Rockhill Papers.

CHAPTER TWELVE

Near East and Far East

Before Rockhill left St. Petersburg, Secretary Knox forwarded a letter of instructions stating that President Taft desired "that the Embassy's energies be constantly directed to the real and commercial rather than the academic interests of the United States in the Near East." "Dollar diplomacy" in the Near East took form in an effort to gain a railroad concession in Turkey for an American company. The Americans failed and Secretary Knox attributed this—up to the time of Rockhill's appointment—to the obstruction of the German Ambassador, Baron Marschall von Bieberstein, and the attitude of the Grand Vizier, Hakki Pasha.[1]

The Taft administration had even less success in Turkey than it did in China. Rockhill assumed his duties as Ambassador to Turkey on August 28, 1911, and shortly afterward the venture of the Ottoman American Development Company came to an end. A few months later, Rockhill wrote to J. V. A. MacMurray in the Department of State:

> This collapse is not encouraging for the Embassy to attempt to take up with the Ottoman Government the subject of any further participation of American financial or industrial enterprise in this country. The Department is very anxious, I know, to extend our relations here; but how the devil are you going to do it if nobody in America, I mean in the business world, is willing to give to the extension of our interests in this country either time or trouble or even to pledge to keep good faith with the people here in case something is given them. I trust that you, in your wisdom, will give me full instructions as to how I am to act here, because I really don't see what we are to do in the matter of carrying out the wishes of our country.[2]

With the collapse of the Ottoman American Development Company, the Taft administration made no further effort to promote American business enterprise in Turkey.

While serving in Turkey, Rockhill witnessed the collapse of the Empire in northern Africa and Europe. Italy, aiming at the conquest of Tripoli, declared war against the Sultanate on September 29, 1911. When Turkey suffered disastrous military defeats resulting in the loss of Tripoli, the Balkan States decided to strike, and declared war against her in October, 1912. Again Turkey met defeat. While the Greeks and Serbians wrested control from the Turks

[1] Secretary of State Philander Knox to W. W. Rockhill, June 17, 1911, Rockhill Papers.

[2] Rockhill to J. V. A. MacMurray, November 6, 1911, Rockhill Papers.

in the Aegean Islands and Macedonia, the Bulgars laid siege to Adrianople and advanced to within twenty miles of Constantinople. In December, 1912, Turkey signed an armistice and peace negotiations were begun; but a month later the Young Turk extremists seized power in Constantinople and quickly renewed hostilities. Suffering the loss of her few remaining positions in Europe, she signed a second armistice in April, 1913. A treaty negotiated the following month limited Turkish control in Europe to Constantinople and its immediate vicinity.

War created a number of problems for the American representative in Constantinople. In the spring and summer of 1912, ships flying the American flag and claiming American protection became the subject of dispute when they violated port rules of the Ottoman government laid down to assure neutrals safe passage through the mined harbor approaches and shore batteries. While ownership of the vessels had been vested in American hands and duly registered with the American government, the transfers were spurious, prompted by the desire to gain the protection of a strong neutral nation.

On April 29, 1912, one of these ships, the *Texas,* owned by the Archipelago-American Line, was sunk in the harbor of Smyrna after a violation of rules and ample warning by Turkish officers. Captain Macris, a Greek subject, was picked out of the water in a semi-conscious state and placed under arrest by the local officials of the Ottoman government. The American Consul-General at Smyrna, George Horton, protested his arrest and imprisonment and claimed that the captain, although a Greek, was subject to American consular jurisdiction. The Ottoman government refused to accept the argument, charging that as the captain was not on the ship when arrested, the ship having sunk, he was subject to its jurisdiction. Turkish lives had been lost as a result of the unlawful action of the captain and the Turks were determined to punish the offender.

Rockhill, always an independent spirit, disagreed with Consul-General Horton and advised the State Department: "With the facts as submitted I do not see my way to support him [Horton], and have instructed him not to commit himself further until categorically instructed, but that he might, without bringing the point to an issue, inform the Governor General that he reserved all rights." [3] The State Department, disagreeing with Rockhill, instructed him to ask the Ottoman authorities to surrender the imprisoned captain.[4] Rockhill replied that he thought it very doubtful that the penal jurisdiction of American consuls could be extended to the captain who was not an American citizen. He warned: "When our right is not clear it is better not to make the claim than to make it and then withdraw." [5] Secretary Knox did not accept this advice and instructed Rockhill to request the surrender of the captain to the jurisdiction of the

[3] Rockhill to Knox, May 5, 1912, Department of State Archives.

[4] Acting Secretary of State Huntington Wilson to Rockhill, May 8, 1912, Department of State Archives.

[5] Rockhill to Knox, May 13, 1912, Department of State Archives.

American Consul-General.[6] This Rockhill did but without success. In November the captain was found guilty by an Ottoman court and sentenced to eighteen months' imprisonment. The State Department was forced to acknowledge defeat.

The war between Turkey and Italy placed Ambassador Rockhill in a position to be of service in the negotiations between the two warring nations. The chaotic situation in Constantinople and the war-weariness and financial difficulties in Rome caused both belligerents to hope for a termination of hostilities. Rockhill was approached late in May, 1912, by Assim Bey, the Turkish Foreign Minister, with a suggestion that the United States mediate. This proposal was rejected but Rockhill entered into a correspondence with the United States Ambassador to Italy, Thomas J. O'Brien. The two American Ambassadors served as media for the exchange of views between the Italian Premier and the Foreign Minister of Turkey. In a minor way this helped bring about the restoration of peace.[7]

When military disaster created the usual problems of displaced peoples and dire human want, Rockhill gave generous assistance. Relief funds raised in the United States were dispensed under his personal supervision. His efforts were recognized by the American Red Cross and by the people of Turkey.[8] From a group of twenty-seven *mohadjers,* he received a note of appreciation.

> We, your humble servants, a family composed of twenty-seven persons who had emigrated to Constantinople in a destitute condition from our own countries on account of the present war, were crowded into a corner of the Ibrahim Pasha mosque at the Silivri Gate, and while we were suffering the worst extremes of want and poverty on account of our being in need both of food and clothing, by the help of Your Highness and Her Highness Your Lady, we have freed ourselves in every way from poverty and misery and have been living comfortably for four or five months under the protection of Your Highness. Thinking that the kindness and generosity of Your Highness and the love to the poor of Your magnanimous wife are deserving of thanks, condescending, as you did, to honor us by coming over to us once or twice a week during that period, simply for the purpose of providing us with food and supplying our needs, without ever heeding snow or rain or the terrible cold that was raging, and in every way abandoning Your comfort, I have the honor and take the liberty, in the name of the twenty-seven poor people in the said mosque who have enjoyed Your goodness, to present You our thanks in the matter.[9]

In March, 1913, Woodrow Wilson was inaugurated President. Rockhill offered his resignation as was customary for all appointees when a new President took office. But this was considered a mere formality and did not mean

[6] Knox to Rockhill, May 29, 1912, Department of State Archives.

[7] William C. Askew, *Europe and Italy's Acquisition of Libya, 1911-1912* (Durham: Duke University Press, 1942), p. 242.

[8] President Woodrow Wilson to Rockhill, December 20, 1913, Rockhill Papers.

[9] Letter from twenty-seven *mohadjers* to Rockhill, March 13, 1913, Rockhill Papers.

that he wished to retire. In May he wrote to a friend in Washington wondering what plans Wilson and Bryan might have for him.[10] In August, Secretary of State William Jennings Bryan wrote: "Although not unmindful of your long and distinguished career both in the foreign field and at home, through certain exigencies the President now desires me to inform you of his acceptance of your resignation of the office of American Ambassador to Turkey." [11] Once again party considerations triumphed over the importance of the foreign service. After a period of almost thirty years with the Department of State, Rockhill had been abruptly dismissed.

In Rockhill's place Wilson appointed Henry Morgenthau, a heavy contributor to the Democratic campaign chest. Strangely, the Democratic party, which had been in office when Rockhill entered the foreign service and which had elevated him to Assistant Secretary of State in 1896, now looked upon him as a Republican because he had continued to serve when that party was in power. The editor of the *Providence Journal* asked: "When will we cease the wretched policy of casting our most useful men in the Diplomatic Service aside in the best years of their public career?" [12] Another editor, reflecting on Bryan's dismissal of the Ambassador, called it intellectual waste and deplored the fact that "our diplomats [are] footballs of politics." [13]

Before Rockhill left Constantinople, President Wilson called for an about-face on "dollar diplomacy" in China. Declining to request the group of American bankers to continue in the banking consortium organized by Willard Straight, the President said that the conditions of the loan made by the consortium seemed to touch the administrative independence of China. Burdensome taxes on the Chinese had been pledged as security and, if the government now asked the bankers to continue, Wilson thought it might eventually be necessary to interfere in the financial and political affairs of China.

This change in policy, based on idealistic considerations for China's welfare, failed to gain Rockhill's complete approval. Well acquainted with the reluctance of the United States to assume responsibilities abroad, he doubted that the American people were prepared to participate in world affairs on the scale contemplated by the Taft administration. However, he recognized the difficulties of promising support to the bankers; public opinion might make it impossible to redeem the promise in some future time of crisis. In a letter to J. V. A. MacMurray, Rockhill wrote of the dilemma facing those responsible for American policy.

---

[10] Rockhill to John Bassett Moore, May 3, 1913, Rockhill Papers.

[11] Secretary of State William Jennings Bryan to Rockhill, August 21, 1913, Rockhill Papers.

[12] Clipping among the Rockhill Papers in the possession of Miss Marion Crutch of Litchfield, Connecticut.

[13] Editorial, "Our Diplomats Footballs of Politics," *Philadelphia Public Ledger,* December 13, 1914, Rockhill Papers in the possession of Miss Crutch.

Of course that policy imposed upon us responsibilities and duties which might become of a very serious nature. Were we, are we or will we ever be—until a radical change has come over us—willing as a country to discharge these duties and responsibilities as we would be expected to by the other foreign Governments participating with us in these undertakings? I see no sign that we will; therefore I am inclined to think that the terminating of the policy of the previous Administration is perhaps well advised, although we may not escape responsibilities by so doing, and may even expose ourselves to greater ones by relinquishing any control over the operations of our capitalists and industrialists in those countries, for, it is of course inconceivable that our Government should not give them support if they get into trouble through financial or other forms of embarrassment in which the countries with which they have entered into business relations may have fallen subsequently thereto.[14]

Eventually the government would have to extend some measure of support to the bankers, although no promises had been made, and yet it would hardly be in a position to make that support effective. In further discussion, Rockhill stated that commerce, politics, and finance formed a trinity, and that no country could put aside one without losing the others. He thought that the Wilson administration must have been lacking in information as to the true condition of affairs in China. So corrupt were the officials of that country that no foreign financiers could possibly risk making a loan without adequate security.

Wilson was more in step with the times than Rockhill. Rockhill's views reflected his experience in nineteenth-century China where Western nations showed scant respect for Chinese sovereignty. A new day had arrived when nationalism made Western political intervention intolerable. Rockhill had absorbed some of the cavalier attitude toward the Oriental so common among Westerners in the treaty ports.

In September, 1913, Rockhill returned to the United States for a brief visit. His plans for the future were uncertain. Now that he had been dismissed from the foreign service and left without a means of livelihood, he considered seeking a position with some business concern that might make use of his knowledge of China. He wrote to acquaintances in this regard. While interested in securing employment eventually, the matter was not pressing. He already had made plans to leave for China in October to see what conditions were like since the revolution of the previous year.

Going by way of Europe, he and Mrs. Rockhill first made a survey of conditions in Outer Mongolia. The extreme backwardness of the people impressed him but he was more concerned with the relations of Russia and China in this borderland. Rockhill wrote that fear of the "yellow peril" had caused Russia to adopt a policy of promoting trade in Mongolia by government aid, but in this she had not been successful due to the natural advantages enjoyed by the

[14] Rockhill to MacMurray, April 11, 1913, Rockhill Papers.

Chinese. Rockhill thought that the best solution was for China and Russia to uphold the autonomy of Outer Mongolia.[15]

Rockhill arrived in Peking in February, 1914, to observe the workings of the Republican government. Until recently he had been pessimistic concerning the success of the new regime. To the American Consul-General at Shanghai, Nelson T. Johnson, he had written: "I am watching with keenest interest the present attempt at representative government in China. I hope it will prove a success, though I cannot imagine one solitary reason for thinking that it will; however, I may be wrong." [16] In a letter to MacMurray, Rockhill was not only pessimistic but critical of the Republican government.

> I cannot but think that if the President and Mr. Bryan had been thoroughly conversant with the real condition of affairs in China, they would never have dreamt of recognizing the Chinese Republic which, as every one knows, has very little authority in China and certainly does not, by the wildest flights of fancy, represent the wishes or desires of even a fraction of the inhabitants of that vast country. However, this recognition will not help the Republic (Thank God! for I am absolutely opposed to its maintenance a day longer than it is necessary) as the President and the Secretary of State seem to think it may. The President and Mr. Bryan evidently imagine that the wild utterances of a few American educated Chinese and foreigners in their employ are the expression of the opinions of the whole nation. This is lamentable nonsense. Commencing with the President of the so-called Republic, he is no more in favor of a Republic in China, nor does any more believe in the possibility of its establishment itself permanently in the country than does the Emperor of all the Russias in the dreams of the pan-slavists and other doctrinaires in his Empire! Business, big business I mean, as it is now understood in America and elsewhere, will not come to us in China when we have sacrificed absolutely our right to express our views and to a certain extent to control the politics of the country.[17]

These views were typical of Westerners who had lived in China. Rockhill, like so many others, had developed a strong attachment for the country; but he had also been witness to the corruption of Chinese officials and a widespread ignorance and indifference concerning political affairs. Because he knew China so well, Rockhill found it difficult to believe that Republicanism would be successful.

His first impression of the new regime on arriving in Peking was unfavorable. He noted in his diary:

> The old story of the conversion of a mud scow into a line-of-battle ship without means or knowledge of how to go about it and the clear foreboding that the new thing may blow up with them without their even knowing in what part of it the

[15] W. W. Rockhill, "The Question of Outer Mongolia," *Journal of the American Asiatic Association,* May, 1914; reprint in Rockhill Papers.

[16] Rockhill to Nelson T. Johnson, April 28, 1913, Rockhill Papers.

[17] Rockhill to MacMurray, April 11, 1913, Rockhill Papers.

danger lies. All the Chinese in public life from the President down are floundering and already beyond their depth. It is a sad plight.[18]

Dr. Paul Reinsch, American Minister in Peking, who ardently advocated the establishment of a democracy similar to that in the United States, was disturbed by the Rockhills' views. He found that Mrs. Rockhill "affected a very reactionary view of things in China, praising the Empire and making fun of all attempts at modernization." Rockhill, Reinsch thought, "was evidently also filled with regret for the old days in China which had passed." [19]

Although sceptical of the success of the Republic, Rockhill was induced to accept the post of general adviser to President Yuan Shih-k'ai. A son of the President, Yuan Yuan-t'ai, asked him to serve, and, on February 11, the President invited him to dinner and urged him to accept the post.[20] Rockhill was permitted to state his own terms, including a salary of $1,000 a month and the understanding that he would reside in the United States.[21]

It may seem strange that Rockhill, who had been so sceptical of the success of the attempt at Republican government in China, should have accepted the position of adviser. It may be that financial considerations influenced his decision, but he may also have reasoned that, the Manchus having abdicated, China's best hope was the Yuan regime. The two men were friends of long standing. Rockhill had been chiefly opposed to Chinese experiments with the Western style of representative government and democracy; as long as the autocratic Yuan remained in control, in spite of avowals of democratic aims, there would be no danger of even futile attempts to impose Western political institutions. Whatever the reason for Rockhill's acceptance, the wily Yuan probably knew the value of a friendly supporter in the United States.

His career as adviser to Yuan Shih-k'ai apparently had little influence on the Republic. During April, Rockhill made a survey of conditions in Canton, Shanghai, and Nanking. In a report to Yuan he spoke favorably of conditions in those areas but urged the necessity of winning the confidence of the moneyed classes and local officials. Rockhill thought the new government must first of all establish its credit by redeeming outstanding issues of paper money. This, he believed, could be done by borrowing money in China—providing the people were assured that the administration was honest. To gain public confidence the government should charter a private bank free from political influence; expert Western accountants should be employed. Rockhill cited Alexander Hamilton's views as the basis for the success of the American Republic in its early years.[22]

[18] Rockhill's diary, entry February 8, 1914, Rockhill Papers.

[19] Paul S. Reinsch, *An American Diplomat in China* (Garden City: Doubleday, Page & Co., 1922), p. 30.

[20] Rockhill's diary, entries for February 3 and 11, 1914, Rockhill Papers.

[21] Rockhill to Yuan Shih-k'ai, March 11, 1914, Rockhill Papers; note written by Rockhill, March 23, 1914, Rockhill Papers.

[22] Rockhill Memorandum to Yuan, May 7, 1914, Rockhill Papers.

On his return to the United States in June, the adviser continued to emphasize the importance of a privately owned national bank as a means of placing the government on a sound financial basis. Yuan expressed sympathy with the proposal but did not adopt it.[23]

Hoping to bring about an improvement in the conditions of foreign trade, Rockhill proposed a program for the abolition of *likin* in return for the remission of indemnity payments arising out of the Boxer settlement. In a memorandum for Yuan, he wrote: "The greatest problem that the Republic has to solve is found in the critical state of the financial situation: a situation that is being aggravated by the necessity of further borrowing from Foreign Powers and of increasing the burden of debt which already amounts to about £160,000,000 sterling." One of the heaviest items was the annual sum to be paid on account of the interest and the amortization of the Boxer indemnity. Rockhill suggested that the central government "negotiate with the Powers for the remission of the balance of the Boxer indemnity, which would enable China to abolish taxation of every kind on goods in transit, including Export Duty on Native goods passing from one Treaty Port to another, Coast Trade Duty, Inward and Outward Transit Dues and Likin." He estimated that the amount of the indemnity payments would approximately equal the revenue from these taxes. Rockhill cited the advantages to be gained by the abolition of *likin.* These taxes, he wrote, increased the cost of goods, hindered trade because of uncertainty as to the amount of the tax, and resulted in delay in the shipment of goods. He added that the collectors of the tax exploited both the government and the merchants. The gain of the foreign powers in the increased trade resulting from the freedom from internal taxation would more than outweigh the losses they would suffer from remission of indemnity payments.[24]

Rockhill advised Yuan that it would be a mistake for the government to abolish *likin* in exchange for an increase in import duties, for, under the Mackay treaty of 1902, the tariff would be set at 12.5 per cent on all goods whether luxuries or necessities. He believed that "the Government would do well to leave the revision of the Import Tariff alone until China is in a position to negotiate a scientific Tariff." To promote foreign trade it would also be necessary to improve railway management and prevent dishonest merchants from destroying "the reputation of Chinese goods by adulteration and other malpractices, such as putting water into Cotton, sand into Camels' wool, Chunen into Ducks' Feathers, Tallow into insect Wax, and so on." [25]

The outbreak of war in August, 1914, added to the difficulties of Yuan's government. Hostilities created so great a demand for money in the Western nations that China was no longer able to borrow abroad. Rockhill had warned

[23] Admiral Ts'ai Ting Kan to Rockhill, May 19, 1914, Rockhill Papers.

[24] Rockhill Memorandum to Yuan entitled "Scheme for the Abolition of Likin, and for all other Taxation on Goods in Transit, in Exchange for the Remission of the Balance of the Boxer Indemnity," Rockhill Papers.

[25] *Ibid.*

that this would happen, and again he urged the necessity of establishing a private bank which would make available to the central government private funds lying idle in China.[26]

Yuan Shih-k'ai and his Cabinet were more concerned about the danger of Japan's making use of the European conflict to seize portions of their territory than they were about financial problems. Faced with this danger, China turned to the United States with a proposal for the neutralization of her territory and adjacent waters. Secretary Bryan gave the plan his support but war spread to the Far East before the warring nations were able to agree on a formula. Japan was determined to enter the conflict in accordance with her interpretation of her duties as an ally of Great Britain. Aware of the dangers to their interests in China, should Japan become a combatant, the British first declined the offer, but on August 7, confronted with a need for additional naval power, they called for Japanese assistance. Japan promptly delivered an ultimatum to Germany, and, on August 23, declared war. Before the end of the month, a Japanese fleet occupied Tsingtao and by the close of the year the province of Shantung was in the hands of the Japanese military.

Rockhill thought the action of Japan in attacking Germany in Shantung quite understandable, "for the strong naval base of Tsing-tao is a menace to Japan and Great Britain, as it is certainly a consistent danger to China." The fact that British troops were fighting as allies of the Japanese in Shantung was reassuring. To Admiral Ts'ai Ting Kan, Yuan's intimate associate, he wrote:

> I fancy that the British Government has received a formal positive pledge from Japan that she will not simply substitute herself for Germany in the leased territory, but will restore the country to China. Personally I am inclined to think that the destruction of German trade competition in China is of infinitely more consequence to the Japanese than the possesssion of Kiao-chau. . . .[27]

Admiral Ts'ai took no such optimistic view. He declared that Japan intended to make of Shantung a second Manchuria.[28]

While in the United States, Rockhill wrote articles for the *Journal of the American Asiatic Association* on conditions in China. In these he emphasized the economic difficulties facing the Republic and the need for restoring confidence among the people in their government. According to him, the policy of Yuan

> aims primarily at the maintenance of peace and order throughout the country and the restoration of confidence among the people in those put over them in authority; it advocates slow, well-reasoned, practical reforms, suited to meet the real and immediate wants of the people and with due recognition of their peculiarities of race and past culture; to the development of agriculture, commerce and industry, and the spread of such education among the masses as will best con-

[26] Rockhill to Ts'ai, August 14, 1914, Rockhill Papers.

[27] Rockhill to Ts'ai, September 9, 1914, Rockhill Papers.

[28] Ts'ai to Rockhill, October 17, 1914, Rockhill Papers.

tribute to that end and to their comprehension of the rights and duties of citizens of a constitutional, modern state, with a representative body.[29]

Rockhill's support of the Republic and his expressions of confidence in the democratic aspirations of Yuan drew caustic comments from J. O. P. Bland. While Bland had agreed in general with Rockhill's views on China, he now took issue with Rockhill and wrote:

But, as regards Yuan himself and his alleged devotion to the Constitution, to the Council of State and all the other steps taken for the befooling of public opinion abroad, *you* know, my dear Rockhill, just as well as I do, that this is "face-pidgin" and in accordance with immemorial precedents of Chinese statecraft, on the good old autocratic lines. . . . Yuan has established a sort of authority—(let us be quite frank about it)—by bribery, bloodshed and gentle arts of assassination. He is maintaining his authority by means of military despotism, backed by the purse, the only remaining power in authority, and his authority will last just so long as the money holds out. . . . Let us re-establish the Dragon Throne, put Yuan upon it (or anyone else you choose), and let him proceed to issue Imperial edicts, handing out flap-doodle to the Stupid People, just as in the old sweet way, world without end, Amen! [30]

The course later followed by Yuan showed that, whether he was a statesman or not, he certainly was no champion of democracy. Before his death in June, 1916, he sponsored a movement for the restoration of monarchy. Though Yuan had considerable support, revolution broke out before he could ascend the throne and he was compelled to give up his plan.

It is doubtful that Rockhill expressed his real views of the Republican regime in China in the articles he wrote for the *Journal of the American Asiatic Association*. In the official employ of the Republic and seeking an American loan for the hard-pressed regime, Rockhill was scarcely in a position to be critical.

The Rockhills spent the summer and fall of 1914 at "Edgehill," their modest but beautifully situated home in Litchfield, Connecticut. It was their intention to spend their years of retirement in this idyllic town high in the Berkshires. Rockhill would spend all of his time with his beloved Chinese books in his own well-ordered library. But Rockhill felt that retirement was not yet at hand. In the fall of 1914, he decided that, as adviser to President Yuan Shih-k'ai, he was needed in Peking. On November 28, he and Mrs. Rockhill sailed from San Francisco.

Before leaving, Rockhill had contracted a cold which developed into a serious attack of pleurisy during the voyage. He went ashore at Honolulu for treatment and, apparently, recovered. But, a few days later, he suffered a heart attack, and, on December 8, 1914, Rockhill died.

After the funeral service in Honolulu, the body was returned to Litchfield

[29] W. W. Rockhill, "Conditions in China as Viewed from Peking," *Journal of the American Asiatic Association,* June, 1914; reprint in Rockhill Papers.

[30] J. O. P. Bland to Rockhill, August 20, 1914, Rockhill Papers.

for burial. A Chinese pine, presented by the Department of Agriculture, marks his grave. The newspaper notices of his death give uniform testimony of the high regard in which Rockhill was held by his own generation. Editorial writers of the great metropolitan dailies and of the small-town weeklies generously acclaimed him as the country's foremost career diplomat and as one of the finest the country had produced. Typical of the comments is that of a writer for the *Galveston News:*

> Most of his service was in the Near and Far East, and by reason of the experience thus gained he came to be recognized as one of the foremost authorities in the world respecting Asiatic problems and policies. Certainly there was no one in this country who rivaled him. There was no one to whom the United States could turn with more confidence for knowledge and suggestion concerning the perplexing matters that concern our relations with the Orient.[31]

Rockhill had become a symbol of the expert and well-trained diplomat whom Americans hoped would some day find a more ready welcome and a more secure tenure in the foreign service.

[31] Clipping among the Rockhill Papers in the possession of Miss Crutch.

CHAPTER THIRTEEN

First and Foremost a Scholar

William Woodville Rockhill served as the prototype of the present-day foreign expert so much in demand since American entry into World War II. Although diplomatic careers were reserved largely for men of wealth long after Rockhill's death—and the qualifications have not yet been wholly altered—he was the first top-rank American diplomat who had made a long and intensive study of a foreign country, its language, history, ethnography, and culture. That as a scholar he should have found such a prominent place in the foreign service must be attributed to fortuitous circumstance and to the willingness of Cleveland, Roosevelt, and Taft to subordinate political considerations, on occasion, to the importance of having qualified men.

While diplomacy certainly benefited by his profound learning in the area of Oriental history, Rockhill was himself an advocate of scholarship for scholarship's sake. When he entered the foreign service, it was primarily to have the opportunity to learn the spoken language of Tibet. During the remainder of his life, no matter how important the diplomatic post, he continued to study and write; the long hours he spent in his library gave him the greatest enjoyment he knew.

Denied a leave of absence for exploration during his first tour of duty at Peking, Rockhill used a brief vacation to go to the Lamasery of Wu-t'ai shan in the province of Shansi. On his return to Peking, he presented a scholarly paper to the local Oriental Society which was published in its journal in January, 1888. In this paper he gave a brief history of this famous Buddhist sanctuary and a report of his observations. He also wrote an article for the *American Oriental Society's Proceedings* on the lamaist ceremony called "making of mani pills" and another entitled "Korea in Its Relations with China" for the *Journal of the American Oriental Society.*

Rockhill's zealous pursuit of Tibetan studies led to his dismissal from the foreign service in 1888. During the next four years he made his two trips of exploration to Mongolia and Tibet and gathered material for two books and several articles. His observations on his first trip were recorded in *The Land of the Lamas*. On his return to the United States after his second trip, Rockhill published a detailed account entitled *Diary of A Journey through Mongolia and Tibet.* Henry Adams, as noted earlier, wrote a warmly appreciative letter scolding Rockhill for his undue modesty: "By the side of your undertakings, all our little literary efforts here are insignificant, and our labor is child-play, yet you make nothing of it." [1]

There was recognition from abroad, too. Early in 1893, Rockhill went to London to receive the Gold Medal of the Royal Geographical Society. Sir Henry Howorth, a leading British geographer, described him as "one of perhaps three men in the world who know both Chinese and Tibetan, and the only man who is known to have waded through the enormous masses of Buddhist literature of Tibet, an absolutely unknown land to all but himself." [2] Another member praised Rockhill as the man who had told him more than anyone else about the religion, politics, habits, and languages of Tibet.

His emphasis on social patterns and institutions foreshadowed the development of the later school of sociology and more particularly the revolutionary work of William Graham Sumner, distinguished professor at Yale University. Rockhill's contemporaries in the United States held to the natural rights philosophy of the Age of Enlightenment. It was still generally believed that democracy as a political ideal had universal validity and that the social forms of Western civilization were absolutes transcending time and locality. Rockhill's findings called in question this entire philosophy. He made it clear that supposedly basic institutions had not always prevailed nor did they now prevail in all societies. When Sumner wrote his classic *Folkways* in 1907, he drew upon Rockhill's writings. Sumner held that what men had assumed to be absolutes were nothing more than customs peculiar to a particular society. While Sumner was indebted to many others, it is nevertheless true that Rockhill's accounts of Mongolia and Tibet contributed greatly to his theory of social relativism.

Although Rockhill accepted a position as Chief Clerk in the State Department in 1893 and advanced rapidly to the position of Assistant Secretary, there was no pause in his studies. He wrote a number of articles based on his trips of exploration, and, in 1896, he published two articles based on new research, "The Dungan Rebellion and the Mohammedans in China" and "Tibetan Buddhist Birth Stories." From this time on he devoted himself to China's early relations with the outside world.

The *American Historical Review* published a paper by Rockhill entitled "Diplomatic Missions to the Court of China. The Kotow Question." The kowtow question was a major obstacle to the establishment of diplomatic relations between the Imperial government and Western nations until well into the nineteenth century. The Chinese and Manchus insisted on foreign envoys performing the kowtow in the presence of the Emperor; Westerners were equally persistent in refusing. Rockhill, revealing his knowledge of Oriental history, traced the difficulty to the difference in the status of envoys in Asiastic

[1] *Letters of Henry Adams,* ed. by Worthington Chauncey Ford (Boston: Houghton Mifflin Co., 1938), II, 63.

[2] Notes on meeting and a paper by Rockhill entitled "A Journey in Mongolia and Tibet," *The Geographical Journal,* III (May, 1894).

and Western countries. According to Western custom, an envoy to a foreign country was the equal of his sovereign while representing him. In the Orient, an envoy enjoyed no more status than a messenger.[3] Rockhill traced the history of diplomatic missions to the court of China from the eighth century to 1894 drawing on his wide acquaintance with medieval sources.

Rockhill's appointment to Greece in 1897, although leading to personal unhappiness, gave him more time to pursue his own scholarly interests and enabled him to bring to completion the editing and translating of *The Journey of William of Rubruck to the Eastern Parts of the World.* This account of a French friar who visited the Mongols in the middle of the thirteenth century, written originally in Latin, had been brought to the attention of modern scholars by the writings of Roger Bacon and later by Richard Hakluyt. Rockhill's translation was the first in any modern language. In an introductory chapter on the sources of information available to William of Rubruck in preparing for the journey, Rockhill discussed the European reactions to the Mongol invasions and reviewed reports by earlier travelers regarding the barbarians who swept through Russia and the Balkans. In editing the account, he drew on medieval Chinese sources comparing the observations of the friar with those of his Chinese contemporaries. According to Rockhill, the friar was a shrewd and cautious observer who made one of the greatest single contributions to Western knowledge of Asia.[4]

[3] W. W. Rockhill, "Diplomatic Missions to the Court of China. The Kotow Question," *American Historical Review* (April and July, 1897), p. 428.

[4] Rockhill wrote: "Let us now note what Friar William was able to add by his journey and careful observations to Europe's sum of general and geographical knowledge. His principal contributions to geographical science were the indication of the true sources and course of the Don and Volga, the lake nature of the Caspian, the identity of Cathay with the classical country of Seres, a description of the Balkash and of the inland basin of which it occupies the eastern extremity, the first description of the city of Karakorum, the first mention of Kaoli or Korea, and of the Tungusic tribes of Orangai, the *Orienguts* of medieval Mohammedan writers. Natural history owes to him the earliest mention in western writers of the wild ass or *kulan,* and of the *argali* or *avis Poli.* Ethnology is indebted to him for interesting facts too numerous to mention. To him linguistics and anthropology owe the first accurate information on the Goths of the Crimean coast, on the identity of the Comans with the Kipchak, Turks and Cangle, on the difference between the Tartars and the Mongols, on the complexity of the languages of the Bashkirds *(Pascatir)* and the Hungarians, on the origin of the Danubian Bulgarians, on the affinity between the languages of the Russians, Poles, Bohemians and Slavs and that of the Wandals, and on that of the Turkish language with that of the Uigurs and Comans. He was the first to give a nearly accurate explanation of the Chinese script, to note the true peculiarities of the Tibetan, Tangutan (Turkish), and Uigur modes of writing. . . . He was the first to describe the Christian communities in the Mongol empire, and to give details of their rituals and the tenets of their faith; we owe to him the earliest description of the Lamas or northern Buddhist monks, of their temples, their ritual, their Living Buddhas, of their use of prayer beads, and their favourite formula, *Om mani padme, hum.*" William of

On his return to the United States in 1899 Rockhill was considered for appointment as Librarian of Congress and had the active support of Theodore Roosevelt. President McKinley succumbed to pressure from Henry Cabot Lodge who was successful in having a disappointed Massachusetts politician named. At almost the same time he was considered by the public libraries of both New York and Boston. He showed no interest in these positions and likewise declined an invitation to become professor of Oriental languages at the University of California. Had these opportunities presented themselves earlier, it is quite possible that Rockhill would never have followed a diplomatic career.

In 1905 Rockhill completed a small volume entitled *China's Intercourse with Korea from the XVth Century to 1895*. It added but little to earlier articles written by Rockhill. While the book lacks completeness and tends to be a legalistic approach to the subject of Sino-Korean relations, it includes translations of several Chinese and Korean documents of importance.[5]

For students of the recent history of China and Korea, Rockhill performed a valuable service in compiling *Treaties and conventions with or concerning China and Korea, 1894-1904* and *Treaties, conventions, agreements, ordinances, etc. relating to China and Korea,* covering the period 1904 to 1908.[6] Rockhill based his selection of documents on his belief that China entered upon a new period of history after the Sino-Japanese War of 1894-1895, and that the many private agreements regarding railroad concessions and mining rights were as important in the relations of China with the outside world as the more formal treaties. J. V. A. MacMurray, whose compilation of treaties and agreements has served as a standard work since its publication in 1919, followed Rockhill's plan and, in acknowledging the aid and encouragement he had received, he dedicated his collection to Rockhill.

Among Rockhill's research projects while Minister to China was a history of the relations between the Dalai Lamas of Tibet and the Manchu emperors of China, a subject suggested to him by his role as adviser to the Dalai Lama during the latter's visit to Peking in 1908. In characteristic manner, he paid great attention to the careful verification of facts, studied scores of Chinese and Tibetan documents and histories, and employed English, French, and Ger-

---

Rubruck, *The Journey of William of Rubruck to the eastern parts of the world, 1253-55, as narrated by himself, with two accounts of the earlier journey of John of Pian de Carpine.* Translated from the Latin, and edited, with an introductory notice, by William Woodville Rockhill (London: The Hakluyt Society, 1900), p. 37.

[5] W. W. Rockhill, *China's Intercourse with Korea from the XVth century to 1895* (London: Luzac & Co., 1905), Preface.

[6] *Treaties and conventions with or concerning China and Korea, 1894-1904, together with various state papers and documents affecting foreign interests,* ed. W. W. Rockhill (Washington: Government Printing Office, 1904); *Treaties, conventions, agreements, ordinances, etc. relating to China and Korea (October, 1904-January, 1908) being a supplement to Rockhill's treaties with or concerning China and Korea,* ed. W. W. Rockhill (Washington: Government Printing Office, 1908).

man secondary works. Although his subject was one of general interest, his treatment is not of appeal to a wide reading public. Only the specialist appreciates his use of Chinese characters in the text itself, his lengthy footnotes analyzing minute details and comparing interpretations of various scholars, and his adamantine refusal to make any concessions to reader appeal. Yet, it must be said that Rockhill was writing for a highly select audience of Sinologues and he achieved what they prize most highly—erudition, disinterested analysis, and clarity.

Also while Minister to China, Rockhill worked on the translating and editing of a Chinese manuscript written in the thirteenth century. Chau Ju-kua, the Chinese author, had served as the inspector of foreign trade in Fukien and in his *Description of Barbarous Peoples* drew upon what he had learned about Southern Asia, Africa, and Europe from sailors and particularly from the Arab seafaring merchants. His book was an invaluable source of information as to the nature of China's commercial relations in the late twelfth and early thirteenth centuries.

Friedrich Hirth, a professor of Chinese at Columbia University, had translated parts of Chau Ju-kua's account in the early 1890's but had laid it aside. When Rockhill manifested an interest in it, Hirth was delighted and, in January, 1904, invited Rockhill to join him in publishing it. While Rockhill commenced working on it at once, it was not completed until 1911, a few months before he left his post at St. Petersburg. The correspondence of the two men shows that Hirth did the first translation and then sent it to Rockhill for his comments. Rockhill wrote the long introduction and the explanatory notes. In the introduction Rockhill surveyed China's relations with the outside world from the time of Alexander the Great down to the twelfth century. Nothing demonstrates Rockhill's thorough and indefatigable scholarship more than this introduction. It is a carefully documented study based on the writings of the ancient Greeks, the Arabs, medieval Europeans, and draws heavily on Chinese dynastic histories. In the explanatory notes, he incorporated critical analysis of the original document, compared collateral accounts in great detail, and ranged over the whole field of German, French, and English historical writing on Chinese subjects. His thoroughness aroused the enthusiasm of Hirth who had been trained in the best German tradition of scientific history.

However fascinating Rockhill and Hirth found the thirteenth-century Chinese description of the barbarians, securing a publisher was no easy task. The use of Chinese characters was essential if the reader was to be able to judge the soundness of the translation, and, since no American firm had Chinese type, a foreign publisher had to be found. The work was finally undertaken by the Imperial Academy of Sciences at St. Petersburg.

The acclaim given the book must have far surpassed the expectations of Rockhill and Hirth. They probably were more interested in gaining the approval of the small coterie of scholars who devoted themselves to Chinese antiquities.

The *New York Times* of Sunday, December 29, 1912, devoted a full page to the highlights of the book. A writer for the *New York Sun,* in a two-column story, said:

> It is not long ago that it was asked with a sneer, "Who reads an American book?" The change is strongly accentuated by the fact that one of the most valuable treasures of Chinese literature has been rescued from forgetfulness by two Americans and that the results of their labors of translation and critical editing have been given to the world by the Imperial Academy of Sciences of St. Petersburg.[7]

In referring to Rockhill, the writer observed that it was in his case that "the Department of State made its first experiment of appointing a foreign Minister on grounds of manifest fitness rather than a reward for political services."

The interest manifested in Chau Ju-kua's *Description of Barbarous Peoples* encouraged Rockhill, then Ambassador to Turkey, to write an article on China's trade during the fourteenth century with southern India, Ceylon, and the countries to the southeast. Rockhill surveyed the nature of the products exchanged, the effect on the Chinese economy, and the policies of the Sung and Yuan dynasties in respect to this foreign trade.

On May 7, 1914, Rockhill, in Shanghai, had addressed the North China Branch of the Royal Asiatic Society on the subject of the sea trade of China under the Yuan and Ming dynasties. Further honor came not long before his death, when Rockhill was elected correspondent of the *Académie des Inscriptions et Belles-Lettres.*

In the diplomatic history of the United States, Rockhill ranks high among those who have played a part in formulating foreign policy. From the time of the writing of the Hay notes until he went to China as Minister in 1905, he wielded a greater influence in the implementation of the Far Eastern policy of the United States than any other man. His understanding of China contributed a great deal to establishing a tradition of friendship between the two countries and shortly after his death the American Asiatic Association, in a memorial volume published in his honor, stated: "No man has ever proved of equal value to the furtherance of American interests in the Far East, and to none of his countrymen has it ever been vouchsafed to be the depository of confidence so unreserved on the part of the rulers of China."

The United States has often relied on men who have had successful careers in business or law to serve in the key posts of its foreign service. Frequently appointments have been made rewards for political services. Rockhill, who faced almost constant financial difficulties because government salaries were inadequate, and whose appointments were never political rewards to a section of the country or to an influential group, learned of the slight value his country placed on highly qualified career diplomats. While he had to make way for

[7] Clipping among the Rockhill Papers in the possession of Miss Marion Crutch of Litchfield, Connecticut.

lesser men due to political exigencies, he never complained on his own behalf but he did labor to improve the lot of those who worked as his subordinates.

The United States, almost four decades after Rockhill's death, occupies a far more important position in world affairs. A new generation of leaders has come to the fore who hope as he did that the American people will be prepared to accept their responsibilities as citizens of a powerful nation. It is equally the hope of the people that decisions in foreign affairs will be entrusted to men with the ability and loyalty of Rockhill.

Bibliography

BOOKS

Adams, Brooks. *America's Economic Supremacy.* New York: Macmillan Co., 1900.

Beresford, Lord Charles. *The Break-Up of China.* New York: Harper & Bros., 1899.

Bland, J. O. P. *Recent Events and Present Policies in China.* Philadelphia: J. B. Lippincott Co., 1912.

Cater, Harold Dean (ed.). *Henry Adams and His Friends: A Collection of His Unpublished Letters.* Boston: Houghton Mifflin Co., 1947.

Clyde, Paul Hibbert. *International Rivalries in Manchuria, 1689-1922.* Columbus: Ohio State University Press, 1926.

Coolidge, Archibald Cary. *The United States As a World Power.* New York: Macmillan Co., 1908.

Croly, Herbert. *Willard Straight.* New York: Macmillan Co., 1924.

De Siebert, B. *Entente Diplomacy and the World: Matrix of the History of Europe, 1909-1914.* Translated by G. A. Schreiner. New York: G. P. Putnam's Sons, 1921.

Dennett, Tyler. *John Hay: From Poetry to Politics.* New York: Dodd, Mead & Co., 1933.

———. *Roosevelt and the Russo-Japanese War: A Critical Study of American Policy in Eastern Asia in 1902-5, Based Primarily upon the Private Papers of Theodore Roosevelt.* Garden City, New York: Doubleday, Page & Co., 1925.

Dennis, Alfred L. P. *Adventures in American Diplomacy, 1896-1906.* New York: E. P. Dutton & Co., 1928.

Faulkner, Harold Underwood. *American Economic History.* 3d ed. New York: Harper & Bros., 1935.

Ford, Worthington Chauncey (ed.). *Letters of Henry Adams.* 2 vols. Boston: Houghton Mifflin Co., 1938.

Griscom, Lloyd C. *Diplomatically Speaking.* New York: Literary Guild of America, Inc., 1940.

Griswold, A. Whitney. *The Far Eastern Policy of the United States.* New York: Harcourt, Brace & Co., 1938.

Harrington, Fred Harvey. *God, Mammon and the Japanese.* Madison: University of Wisconsin Press, 1944.

Hishida, Seiji G. *The International Position of Japan as a Great Power.* New York: Columbia University Press, 1905.

Jessup, Philip C. *Elihu Root.* 2 vols. New York: Dodd, Mead & Co., 1938.

Joseph, Philip. *Foreign Diplomacy in China, 1894-1900: A Study in Political and Economic Relations with China.* London: George Allen & Unwin, Ltd., 1928.

Langer, William L. *The Diplomacy of Imperialism, 1890-1902.* Vol. I. New York: Alfred A. Knopf, Inc., 1935.

Latourette, Kenneth Scott. *The Chinese: Their History and Culture.* 2 vols. New York: Macmillan Co., 1943.

Lewis, Alfred Henry (ed.). *A Compilation of the Messages and Speeches of Theodore Roosevelt, 1901-1905.* Washington: Bureau of National Literature and Art, 1905.

MacMurray, J. V. A. (ed.). *Treaties and Agreements with and concerning China, 1894-1919.* 2 vols. New York: Oxford University Press, 1921.

MacNair, Harley Farnsworth. *China in Revolution: An Analysis of Politics and Militarism under the Republic.* Chicago: University of Chicago Press, 1931.

Millard, Thomas F. *America and the Far Eastern Question.* New York: Moffat, Yard & Co., 1909.

———. *The New Far East: An Examination into the New Position of Japan and Her Influence upon the Solution of the Far Eastern Question.* New York: Charles Scribner's Sons, 1906.

Morse, Hosea Ballou and Harley Farnsworth MacNair. *Far Eastern International Relations.* Boston: Houghton Mifflin Co., 1931.

Nevins, Allan. *Henry White: Thirty Years of American Diplomacy.* New York: Harper & Bros., 1930.

Ogg, Frederic Austin. *Economic Development of Modern Europe.* New York: Macmillan Co., 1917.

Parsons, William Barclay. *An American Engineer in China.* New York: McClure, Phillips & Co., 1900.

Pringle, Henry F. *Theodore Roosevelt.* New York: Harcourt, Brace & Co., 1931.

Records of the General Conference of the Protestant Missionaries of China held at Shanghai, May 7-20, 1890. Shanghai: American Presbyterian Mission Press, 1890.

Reid, John Gilbert. *The Manchu Abdication and the Powers, 1908-1912: An Episode in Pre-War Diplomacy.* Berkeley: University of California Press, 1935.

Reinsch, Paul S. *An American Diplomat in China.* Garden City, New York: Doubleday, Page & Co., 1922.

Rockhill, William Woodville. *China's Intercourse with Korea from the XVth Century to 1895.* London: Luzac & Co., 1905.

———. *Diary of A Journey through Mongolia and Tibet in 1891 and 1892.* Washington: Smithsonian Institution, 1894.

———. *The Land of the Lamas: Notes of A Journey through China, Mongolia, and Tibet.* New York: Century Co., 1891.

——— (ed). *Treaties and conventions with or concerning China and Korea, 1894-1904, together with various state papers and documents affecting foreign interests.* Washington: Government Printing Office, 1904.

——— (ed). *Treaties, conventions, agreements, ordinances, etc. relating to China and Korea (October, 1904-January, 1908) being a supplement to Rockhill's treaties with or concerning China and Korea, 1894-1904.* Washington: Government Printing Office, 1908.

Sandmeyer, Elmer Clarence. *The Anti-Chinese Movement in California.* Urbana: University of Illinois Press, 1939.

Steiger, George Nye. *China and the Occident: The Origin and Development of the Boxer Movement.* New Haven: Yale University Press, 1927.

Stephenson, George M. *A History of American Immigration, 1820-1924.* Boston: Ginn & Co., 1926.

Tansill, Charles Callan. *The Foreign Policy of Thomas F. Bayard, 1885-1897.* New York: Fordham University Press, 1940.

Thomson, H. C. *China and the Powers: A Narrative of the Outbreak of 1900.* New York: Longmans, Green & Co., 1902.

Treat, Payson J. *Diplomatic Relations between the United States and Japan, 1895-1905.* Palo Alto, California: Stanford University Press, 1938.

———. *The Far East: A Political and Diplomatic History.* New York: Harper & Bros., 1928.

Vagts, Alfred. *Deutschland und die Vereinigten Staaten in der Weltpolitik.* Vol. II. New York: Macmillan Co., 1935.

William of Rubruck. *The Journey of William of Rubruck to the Eastern Parts of the World.* Translated by W. W. Rockhill. London: The Hakluyt Society, 1900.

Williams, Edward Thomas. *China Yesterday and Today.* New York: Thomas Y. Crowell Co., 1932.

Willoughby, Westel W. *Foreign Rights and Interests in China.* 2 vols. Rev. ed. Baltimore: The Johns Hopkins Press, 1927.

Zabriskie, Edward H. *American-Russian Rivalry in the Far East.* Philadelphia: University of Pennsylvania Press, 1946.

ARTICLES

"A Russian Appeal for American Good Will," *New York Sun,* July 4, 1899, p. 6.

Conant, Charles A. "The Struggle for Commercial Empire," *The Forum,* XXVII (June, 1899), 427-40.

Crist, David S. "Russia's Far Eastern Policy In The Making," *Journal of Modern History,* XIV (September, 1942), 317-41.

Foster, John W. "The Chinese Boycott," *The Atlantic Monthly,* XCVII (1906), 118-27.

Hippisley, Alfred E. "William Woodville Rockhill," *Journal of the Royal Asiatic Society of Great Britain,* XLVII (April, 1915), 367-74.

"Into the Heart of China," *New York Sun,* June 4, 1899, p. 3.

Livermore, Seward W. "American Naval-Base Policy in the Far East, 1850-1914," *The Pacific Historical Review,* XIII (June, 1944), 113-35.

Lodge, Henry Cabot, "Our Blundering Foreign Policy," *The Forum,* XIX (March, 1895), 8-17.

Millard, Thomas F. "The New China," *Scribner's Magazine,* XXXIX (February, 1906), 240-50.

Moffett, Samuel F. "Ultimate World Politics," *The Forum,* XXVII (August, 1899), 665-68.

Munro, Dana G. "American Commercial Interests in Manchuria," *The Annals,* XXXIX (January, 1912), 154-68.

Notes on meeting and a paper by W. W. Rockhill entitled "A Journey in Mongolia and in Tibet," *The Geographical Journal,* III (May, 1894), 357-88.

Rockhill, William Woodville. "Among the Mongols of the Azure Lake," *Century,* XIX (January, 1891), 350-61.

———. "An American in Tibet. An Account of a Journey Through an Unknown Land. Through Northern China to Koko-nor," *Century,* XIX (November, 1890-March, 1891), 3-17, 250-63, 350-61, 599-606, 720-30.

———. "Conditions in China in 1914 as Viewed from Peking," *Journal of the American Asiatic Association,* XIV (June, 1914), 141-48.

———. "Diplomatic Missions to the Court of China. The Kotow Question," *American Historical Review,* II (April and July, 1897), 427-42, 627-43.

———. "Driven Out of Tibet. An Attempt to Pass from China through Tibet into India," *Century,* XXV (April, 1894), 877-94.

———. "Northern Tibet and the Yellow River," *Century,* XIX (February, 1891), 599-606.

———. "Notes on the Relations and Trade of China with the Eastern Archipelago and the Coasts of the Indian Ocean during the Fourteenth Century," *T'oung Pao,* XIV (1913), 473-76.

———. "The Border-land of China. A Journey Through an Unknown Land," *Century,* XIX (December, 1890), 250-63.

———. "The Dalai Lamas of Lhasa and Their Relations with the Manchu Emperors of China, 1644-1908," *T'oung Pao,* XI (1910), 1-104.

———. "The Question of Outer Mongolia," *Journal of the American Asiatic Association,* XIV (May, 1914), 102-09.

———. "The United States and the Future of China," *The Forum,* XXIX (May, 1900), 324-31.

———. "Through Eastern Tibet and Central China," *Century,* XIX (March, 1891), 720-30.

"William Woodville Rockhill," *National Cyclopedia of American Biography,* VIII, 129.

PUBLIC DOCUMENTS

Congressional Record (1898). Washington: Government Printing Office, 1898.

U.S. Bureau of the Census. *Thirteenth Census of the United States: 1910. Abstract of the Census.* Washington: Government Printing Office, 1913.

U.S. Bureau of Statistics. *Statistical Abstract of the United States: 1900.*

U.S. Congress, Senate. *Treaties, Conventions, International Acts, Protocols, and Agreements between the United States of America and Other Powers, 1776-1909.* Compiled by William M. Malloy, Senate Doc. No. 357, 61st Cong., 2d Sess. Vol. I. Washington: Government Printing Office, 1910.

U.S. Department of Commerce and Labor. *Report of the Secretary of Commerce and Labor: 1906.* Washington: Government Printing Office, 1907.

U.S. Department of State. *Papers Relating to the Foreign Relations of the United States* (1896-1914). Washington: Government Printing Office.

UNPUBLISHED MATERIAL

Hay, John. Collection in Division of Manuscripts, Library of Congress.

Knox, Philander C. Collection in Division of Manuscripts, Library of Congress.

Rockhill, Dorothy. An Account of Her Father's Early Life. Original manuscript is in the possession of Courtland Hoppin, grandson of W. W. Rockhill.

Rockhill, W. W. Collection in Sterling Library, Yale University.

Roosevelt, Theodore. Collection in Division of Manuscripts, Library of Congress.

U.S. Department of State Archives, 1904-1910.

Index